PILC

This is a creative and timely contribution, putting today's Christians in touch with historic spirituality.

Rob Frost rightly reminds us to take time over developing our relationship with God.

His proposals help us to move from the traditional evangelical strength of individual devotion to the less developed art of mutual encouragement in faith and worship.

Those who take up the challenge of this book will find refreshment and growth.

John Earwicker
Prayer Secretary, Evangelical Alliance

This simple style of writing in this book combines with the author's own life experiences, his personal reflections on Scripture, and very apt illustrations from a variety of sources. The reader is invited to enter reflectively into some of the great themes of Christian spirituality.

This invitation is addressed both to church groups and individuals, and takes the form of a journey to explore God's relationship with our world.

> and the end of all our exploring
> will be to arrive where we started
> And to know the place for the first time
> *TS Eliot, Little Gidding, The Four Quartets*

The stages of the journey enable us to reflect on our journey with God.

Rob Frost shows the reader that theology and spirituality are grounded in the issues of life, while the vision leads to the Lord. He shares his own reflections as an encouraging 'fellow pilgrim'.

Brother Benedict Foy, fsc
St Cassian's Centre, Newbury

Pilgrims, and the prayer pilgrimage envisaged, fit the present mood of ecumenical exploration very well indeed. The book will be an excellent tool for those leading imaginative events, as well as encouraging personal prayer adventures.

Mary Holliday
Methodist minister involved in retreats and ecumenical spirituality

Another practical, down-to-earth approach to a deeply spiritual matter from a man who is in touch with the grass roots' desire to meet with God.

Rob offers here another example of his desire to liberate elements of the Christian faith which are locked in the past.

David Martin
National Secretary, Methodist Association of Youth Clubs

By the same author:

Big Questions
Break Me, Shape Me
Breaking Bread
Conversation Starters
Go for Growth
People at Work
Visions

Pilgrims

Going on a pilgrimage today

ROB FROST

KINGSWAY PUBLICATIONS
EASTBOURNE

First published 1990
Reprinted 1990

Front cover photo: The Image Bank

British Library Cataloguing in Publication Data

Frost, Rob
Pilgrims.
1. Christian pilgrimages
I. Title
248.4'63

ISBN 0-86065-814-7

Printed in Great Britain for
KINGSWAY PUBLICATIONS LTD,
1 St Anne's Road, Eastbourne, E Sussex BN21 3UN by
Richard Clay Ltd, Bungay, Suffolk
Typeset by J&L Composition Ltd, Filey, North Yorkshire

To Richard and Janet Baxendale for providing a 'place of retreat' for me at Hall Farm, Brierley.

Acknowledgements

With thanks to: Jacqui Frost (cover) and David Palmer (line drawings) for artwork. The Cheam youth group for their initial enthusiasm and support. The Pilgrims' support group, an ecumenical working party who thrashed out some basic principles. Meryl Smith for typing the final manuscript. Marian Arthur for project co-ordination. The Pilgrims' mission team who are travelling thousands of miles to train pilgrimage leaders. Ralph Ward and Stripes Theatre Company for their support in the allied 'Pilgrims' musical' project.

Contents

Introduction 9
1 The Road to Peace 11
2 Walking with the Lord 29
3 Seed Faith 45
4 The Wilderness Experience 63
5 A View of the World 81
6 The Pilgrim Community 101
7 The Road to the Cross 119
8 Destinations 135
Pilgrim Song 153

Introduction

Welcome to the pilgrimage!

If you've never been on a pilgrimage I hope that the material in this book will stimulate you to go on one.

There are many different kinds of pilgrimage but the purpose of this one is to strengthen your prayer life and it can follow almost any route you choose.

There are three different ways of using this book, and I hope that you might explore all three of them.

(1) A mental pilgrimage

The main chapters introduce the idea of pilgrimage and suggest various themes which can be explored. Everyone can read these chapters.

They are designed to help you make a pilgrimage in your mind.

Pause as you read, picture the different scenes described, and if you feel challenged by the text turn to prayer. If you are housebound and unable to join a group as they walk, you could use these chapters to make a mental pilgrimage in your own home.

(2) A church pilgrimage
At the end of each chapter there is a detailed plan to help you organise a church pilgrimage. The ideas have been tried and tested with a diverse age range and they should provide a stimulating base for any church or youth fellowship pilgrimage.

You don't have to follow the itinerary in the order described in this book. You may care to rearrange the order to suit the geography of the area your group is walking in. There may be too much material for one pilgrimage, so be prepared to leave sections out if you wish. This material would be an ideal basis for a residential conference, church weekend, or series of summer study evenings.

(3) A personal pilgrimage
If you would like to make a personal pilgrimage without a group there are also ideas and activities to help you. If you have been on a church pilgrimage you may care to use this section as a personal follow-up a few weeks or months afterwards.

The material could form the basis of eight different 'Quiet Times' or a day-long pilgrimage on your own.

Whichever kind of pilgrimage you make, I hope and pray that this book will help you to find a deeper prayer life and a closer relationship with the Lord.

I
The Road to Peace

The journey starts

Some sociologists believe that pilgrimages have something in common with the package holidays which are so popular today. Both offer a journey away from everyday life and routine, and the opportunity to view familiar things from a safe distance.

As we begin our 'pilgrimage' it's important that we grasp the value of 'distancing' ourselves from everyday routine. We must leave behind the cares of 'life back home' and make a journey of discovery with the Lord. Our pilgrimage may take many weeks or just a few hours, but it should give us the opportunity to detach ourselves from the pressures of life. It may take us a few miles or across whole continents, but it should enable us to see things from a different perspective.

And so we leave behind our 'Walkmans' and sever ourselves from the chatter of the world, for we need to hear the sound of silence. We distance ourselves from the thoughts that usually fill our minds, and focus on things more permanent than the jottings in our 'Filofax'.

By distancing ourselves from everything familiar we are following in the footsteps of Abraham. His pilgrimage meant leaving everything behind in the search for a new country. He was leaving the relatives he loved and the place where his family had lived successfully for generations; all because he believed God's promise that something better was waiting for him at the end of his journey. It must have been painful to make such a new beginning at the ripe old age of seventy-five.

In medieval times pilgrims knew what it was to distance themselves from everyday life. When they set off on the pilgrim trail they took their lives in their hands. Travelling to holy places in England and overseas was a dangerous business, and they faced the prospect of robbery, shipwreck, fever and even death on their journey. It was quite normal for pilgrims in these times to set their financial affairs in order and make a will before they left. When they went on pilgrimage they knew they might be leaving for ever.

Journeys aren't usually as difficult or as dangerous today, but the modern pilgrim should still strive to leave the distractions of everyday routine and seek for higher things. Perhaps this is harder for our generation than for any previous one because we are so addicted to the buzz of our noisy world.

On this journey we need to make the space to rise above the things that often fill our minds. As we breathe fresh air and walk new paths we must free our minds to think fresh thoughts and glimpse new horizons. We need to take pilgrimage seriously if it is to have more meaning than a pleasant afternoon stroll.

On each of the eight stages on our pilgrimage we are

going to explore a different kind of prayer. In the opening section we are going to think about meditation and experience it for ourselves. In order to meditate we need to learn how to distance ourselves from the pressures of everyday life and to fix our minds on God's word. If we are preoccupied with other things we cannot possibly meditate.

I have had some disastrous experiences of meditation. Perhaps I have an overactive mind, but very often I have found that 'times of meditation' in a service have been an opportunity for my mind to focus on anything but the presence of the Lord. Sometimes I have been in church services where we have been asked to meditate on some object like a candle, but we've been given no clear direction for our thoughts to follow. I tend to end up thinking about candles rather than the Lord.

For me, the most effective kind of meditation is when I fix my mind on the word of God, and concentrate on some passage of Scripture which is rich in meaning and which has a direct bearing on my Christian life. If I look at a candle as I meditate on the words 'Jesus said, "I am the light of the world"', I begin to discover those words coming to life in new ways for me. My mind is focused on the word, not the symbol.

For the first stage of our pilgrimage we will meditate on the profound words of Jesus found in Luke 12. Just one of the following verses will probably give us enough to think about during our time of meditation.

> Aren't five sparrows sold for two pennies? Yet not one sparrow is forgotten by God, so do not be afraid; you are worth much more than many sparrows!

> Look how the wild flowers grow; they don't work or make clothes for themselves. But I tell you that not even King Solomon with all his wealth had clothes as beautiful as one of these flowers.
>
> It is God who clothes the wild grass — grass that is here today and gone tomorrow, burnt up in the oven. Won't he be all the more sure to clothe you? How little faith you have. . . . Be concerned with his kingdom, and he will provide you with these things.

With our minds firmly fixed on one of these verses, we begin to look at the signs of creation all around us and to gather grass and leaves from the hedgerow as we walk. (It's probably best to look at the flowers rather than pick them: we don't want to destroy our environment!) We gather anything, in fact, that symbolises God's care for his creation and his intimate knowledge of all that he has made.

Such things as a bird's feather, a piece of moss, a fallen branch or some different kinds of grass are all suitable symbols. Walking alone, and picking up these fragments of creation, we use them to help us meditate on these powerful words of the Lord.

It's important that as we stoop to look at these things, and maybe pick them up, that they are a means of drawing us closer to the Lord and not an end in themselves. True meditation leads us beyond what we are looking at and into the presence of the Lord. These things are a means of prayer, not an end in themselves.

For me one of the greatest joys of meditation is the sense of surprise and discovery when some aspect of the gospel lights up in a way that's 'just for me'. So there is no 'agenda' for us to follow as we collect these fragments of creation, just an openness to hear the word and apply it to our own particular stressful situations in life.

This passage from Luke 12 really 'lit up' for me in a powerful way when I was very run down emotionally and spiritually. I'd been touring twenty towns with the musical presentation 'Visions' and had been carrying a heavy weight of responsibility. The seven-week tour had been one of the busiest I'd ever known. The stress of speaking to large crowds of people night after night and the lengthy counselling which followed each presentation had really worn me down.

The hectic weeks of travel, the demands of managing a touring team, and the constant exposure to new people in new situations had made me tense and nervous. My patience had evaporated and I'd become increasingly difficult to live with. I'd reached the stage where I was actually finding it hard to relax at all.

Even when the tour had finished my state of mind didn't improve. I couldn't seem to unwind and I found that I couldn't relax by watching my favourite TV programmes or by reading magazines. I kept drifting back to my desk to work when I should have been taking time off to rest. I'd also become dithering and indecisive and I was finding it hard to make the simplest of decisions. I had so much to do that I'd taken to compiling lists for everything. Even sleep was a problem. Although I could fall asleep quite quickly, I would wake up in the early hours to brew tea and mull things over.

My whole body had become a tense, nervous knot. In only a matter of weeks it seemed that I'd forgotten how to relax and even how to laugh. I'd seen these symptoms so clearly in the lives of others, but never so obviously in my own life. I knew that I needed to take note of some of the advice I'd given to others, and to tackle the stress that was twisting me up. For the first time I really understood how it felt to be 'under stress'.

My wife didn't so much suggest that we took a holiday, she insisted on it! We saw an advert in the paper which talked of 'Bargains in Greece' and twelve hours later we were boarding a plane at Gatwick bound for a tiny island called Lesbos. What happened on that holiday was more than a cheap week in the sun — for me it had all the quality of a pilgrimage.

Early on during the holiday, we set out on the serious business of sightseeing. I wasn't very excited at the prospect of a full day away from the island, but the courier assured us that it was a trip not to be missed. So we took the boat across to Turkey and were taken by coach to the ancient city of Pergamum.

Eventually we arrived at a site where archaeologists had uncovered the world's oldest hospital. It was fascinating to walk along pathways where patients took the air more than two-thousand years ago. As I walked beside the ruined wards I felt mysteriously connected to the past.

Our guide explained that much of the treatment was aimed at stress-related illness, and that many of the therapies were designed to help the ancient Greeks relax. Mud baths, role play, exercise and entertainment in the amphitheatre were all used to help them unwind.

I smiled as I realised that people have been trying to find a cure for stress since ancient times. I also found it hard to believe that many of today's most radical treatments are in fact so old. I recognised that I didn't want to live my life like a tightly coiled spring, but I also knew that these remedies were not the ultimate answer to my problems of stress.

Soon after this I sat alone on a small terrace and allowed the tranquility of the scene to wash over me. I gazed across at the beautiful blue bay, the gently sloping olive groves and the misty azure sky. And all around was the distant whirr of crickets. I opened my Bible and read Christ's words from Luke 12.

They were words that I knew well and had often quoted in my preaching . . . but there was a new power in them that day. I felt that God was speaking them just to me.

I took this chapter as the theme for my devotions for the week, and wherever I went I felt the Lord speaking to me through it. Previously I had given these words of Jesus my intellectual assent, but that week I began to apply them practically to my everyday life. As I meditated on the passage I discovered gems of truth which I am still applying several years later.

Jesus didn't speak these words in a vacuum, they were his manifesto to a people under stress. He had just warned them of the things to come, and told them that he would be crucified and that they would be persecuted. They must have felt desperate. How would they defend themselves before synagogues and governors, and how would they cope with persecution and humiliation? Jesus was talking to real people with real problems — people who knew sleepless nights, worries about the future and the fear of the unknown. He was also talking to me.

As I walked around that beautiful Greek island I stopped to stare at the whirling seagulls by the seashore, the red poppies in the olive grove and the different grasses in the meadow, and I found the teaching of Jesus leaping to life.

I'd never been very good at meditation, but that week as I strolled down country lanes and clambered over rocky beaches I found that the things I saw were helping me to explore the meaning of this wonderful passage.

One hot day during our holiday, my wife and I and our

two boys drove out into the country well off the tourist track. There were no road signs, let alone souvenir shops — just an old farmer working a field with a horsedrawn plough.

We were looking for an ancient monastery which we'd heard was open to the public. We entered the main gate, ambled down a long shady verandah and found the tomb of the early church leader called Saint Ignatius. We gazed with wonder at the beautiful scrolls near his tomb, some of which dated back fifteen-hundred years.

As we strolled around this ancient monastery, I sensed the eternal nature of my heavenly Father. I began to see my life in the perspective of God's vast purposes and my work as but a fragment of God's immense design. As I meandered round this shady courtyard I was overwhelmed by a sense of God's greatness and my own insignificance.

But then I looked down and saw the figure of a tiny dead sparrow. Immediately Christ's words confronted me: 'Aren't five sparrows sold for two pennies? Yet not one sparrow is forgotten by God . . . so do not be afraid; you are worth much more than many sparrows.'

In an instant I glimpsed the vastness of my heavenly Father's love, and I saw that his care for all that he has made spans undimmed across the centuries. For this is the God who cares about sparrows. I found the concept mind-blowing. That tiny lifeless body conveyed God's love for me more powerfully than the most eloquent sermon. As I knelt and looked at the dead sparrow I sensed God's intimate care for my insignificant little life in a new and deeper way.

I felt enfolded by the love of God. I recognised again that there was no part of me outside his knowledge and care. There was no aspect of my life he didn't understand and no insecurity of which he was unaware. As I looked at the sparrow I recognised that my every breath was a gift of God and that my being was somehow bound up with his. This sense of the Lord's boundless care flooded over me like a healing stream and I was freed from my spiral of stress and worry.

When we are wrapped up with worry we can lose sight of the Lord's enfolding love for us. We may be worn down by responsibilities at home or at work, or concerned about our own health or future, but a rediscovery of the powerful love of Jesus can bring a stream of renewal into our lives which can change the way we look at things.

A few days later I began to reflect on the words: 'Look how the wild flowers grow; they don't work or make clothes for themselves. But I tell you that not even King Solomon with all his wealth had clothes as beautiful as one of these flowers'.

I certainly didn't feel like a wild flower. As I looked back across my hectic schedule of the previous weeks and remembered the strain and the sleepless nights I pictured myself more like a dried-up weed!

The next day I sat and gazed down at the olive groves, and was impressed by the bright-red poppies which clustered among the trees. As I gazed at the poppies before me I slowly began to understand what Jesus meant. They glowed with colour in the spring sunshine, but made no sound. They weren't struggling and straining, muttering or complaining — they just bloomed.

'Look how the wild flowers grow.' They just absorb the light, the dew and the warmth — and they bloom. As I sat and watched the poppies, I saw that I had been struggling too much in my life, and not spending enough time just enjoying the light and love of Christ. I had been giving out and not spending enough time alone with the Lord.

I saw in a new way that the most important aspect of my Christian witness was not what I did, but what I was. I needed to wilt less and bloom more! And I vowed to spend more time in the Lord's presence each day, and to seek a deeper relationship with him when I returned home.

There and then I bathed in the radiance and love of Christ, and felt my whole being renewed and made whole again. The words of Maclaren sum up how I felt: 'Whoever is able to say to himself "I am" will never know rest until he can turn to God and say "Thou art", and then, laying His hand in the great Father's hand, venture to say "we are".'

The fishing village near where we were staying in Greece was not commercialised. The gentle pattern of daily life continued as it must have done for centuries. Early each morning the fishermen would return with their catch and sell it to those who gathered by the quayside.

Later in the day the farmers would bring their produce into the market square and sell it from makeshift tables. Sheep and cattle were herded through the town on their way to market, and each morning the street bars were crowded with locals deep in conversation. Every afternoon the place was deserted for siesta; and each night the streets were crowded as people gathered to greet each other and talk.

This daily cycle of business and conversation was regular and reassuring. It was all so different from the rush hours, traffic jams and brief greetings of my life in London. I stopped and gazed at this tightly knit community. There was no rat-race here. There was a gentler pace, a greater sense of caring — and fewer trappings of the consumer society. I felt a tinge of jealousy, for in this simpler lifestyle there seemed more space simply to be.

> 'It is God who clothes the wild grass—grass that is here today and gone tomorrow, burnt up in the oven. Won't he be all the more sure to clothe you? How little faith you have! . . . Be concerned with his kingdom, and he will provide you with these things.'

From this faraway place I looked back at the hectic lifestyle that I was trapped in, and saw more clearly just how empty much of it really was. Away from my daily round of meetings and appointments, I could see more clearly the things that were really important.

From that vantage point my material possessions seemed less important, and my relationships more valuable. As I walked through the olive groves I looked at the rough tufts of grass, some of them dried out by the sun. Grass that was a lush green one day but dead the next. This was the natural cycle of things: there is only permanence in God himself.

Much of our rat-race is rooted in vanity. Erich Fromm, writing of the emptiness within our consumer society, concluded. 'In the having mode "it" and "I" have become things. I have "it" because I have the force to make it mine. But there is also a reverse relationship, it has me, because my sense of identity rests upon me having "it".'

As I watched the fishing boats chugging in with seagulls whirling overhead, meandered through the street markets and kicked pebbles on the beach, I began to adjust to a slower pace of life. And as I looked at the transient dying grasses of the field I saw that some of the things I'd valued weren't really important at all. I recognised that much of my inner turmoil had been caused by my desire to live in the kingdoms of this world rather than the kingdom yet to come.

Many of us have been chasing the idols of this world, and have lost our hold on the important values of God's kingdom. As we wander along on our pilgrimage and collect pieces of grass by the wayside, it's good to reflect on the permanence of God's love and the eternal quality of his kingdom.

Luke 12 has so much to say to our generation, and if we are making a pilgrimage with a group it would be good to gather together at the end of this section to share our thoughts and discover all the different insights which the group has discovered during their time of meditation.

Perhaps some of these insights will change our attitudes and give us a new order of priorities long after our pilgrimage is over. At the end of my cut-price holiday in the sun, I shepherded my family through the crowded terminal at Gatwick Airport and pushed my trolley into the cold spring air. But there was no big 'let down' as I returned to work again. The sun-tan soon wore off, but the insights from my meditation still remain.

Organising a church pilgrimage

Route One: from the commissioning point to the nature display.
Aim: to encourage people to discover the joy of meditation and thanksgiving.

Pilgrimage is the kind of activity which the whole church family can enjoy. The route should be suitable for children as well as adults, and it should be as accessible

to those who are elderly or in wheelchairs as to those who are expert ramblers.

An ideal pilgrim group should number between twenty and thirty people, and each group should have one leader. It is important that there are also three or four 'pastors' who have received some training, and who can support the leader and offer friendship and encouragement to the pilgrims.

If there are any children in the group, at least one 'pastor' should be designated to care for them, and to ensure that the activities are made understandable. Although it is best if the children remain with the whole group most of the time, it might be good for them to pray together at times as a subgroup.

In any advance publicity it's important to assure people that this will not be a 'heavy' or 'threatening' experience, but that it has more purpose than a church ramble. As well as sharing details about the route to be taken and what to bring, it would also be helpful if the group had some biblical material to help them prepare for the pilgrimage.

The aim of the pilgrimage is to enrich the devotional life of the whole church and its individual members. It's important that the church looks toward the event prayerfully and with anticipation.

The walk could be held on a Saturday, Sunday or Bank Holiday afternoon, and it would be helpful if everyone gathered at church for lunch before setting off. This would provide a good opportunity for 'breaking the ice' and making sure that everyone knew each other and was open to one another.

At the start of the pilgrim trail there could be a short prayer of 'commissioning', asking the Lord to bless the pilgrimage. During the first section the group talk informally together as they walk. They may care to share together some of the pressures of the past week which they are leaving behind as they start the pilgrimage.

It's surprising how little we know about the people we sit beside each week at church. If this short journey is going to be a meaningful time we need to share a little of who we are and where we're at. It's particularly important that any newcomers to the group are made to feel welcome.

At a suitable point the pilgrim leader reads one or two selected verses from Luke 12:24–31 and encourages the group to focus on these words during a time of silence. Each person walks alone, meditating on the reading and stopping to take in the wonders of creation around them. They collect such things as leaves, twigs or feathers. The important thing about these natural fragments is not quantity but quality. Just one or two items per person may well be sufficient.

As the pilgrims walk alone they may pause in silence to look at other aspects of creation such as wild flowers or birds, and to remember that the Lord's compassion extends beyond these things to enfold them as well. Meditation on this theme for just a few moments should fill our hearts with praise and thanksgiving.

After a few moments of silence the group are called back together, and each pilgrim takes their symbols and lays them on a flat surface like a tree stump. The whole collection is arranged neatly.

As the group stand in a circle around their nature display they hold hands as an act of fellowship and different people share the thoughts that came to them during their meditation.

The group then turns to prayer while keeping their eyes open and looking at the nature display. Different people in the group share some short phrases of praise and thanksgiving. The time of worship and thanksgiving at the nature display could end with some simple praise songs.

Organising a personal pilgrimage

Meditation

Very often we burst into God's presence, say too much and listen too little. Meditation gives us the opportunity to hear what the Lord wants to say to us through his word. It also enables us to quieten our hearts and minds and to concentrate on the Lord, so it is a good preparation for other kinds of prayer.

Preparation

Read through Luke 12 and pick out the verse or phrase you wish to meditate on. It would be good to repeat this phrase over and over again until the meaning really has become clear.

Activity

To collect grass, leaves and other fragments of creation as you walk, pausing to look at things and to touch and feel each item collected. Look carefully at colours and textures, and note sounds like birdsong or the scent of flowers. Keep the Bible verse uppermost in your mind throughout.

Practical advice

(1) Find a quiet place where you won't be disturbed, and as you walk or stop to look at things, let your body relax.
(2) Allow the meaning of the scripture to penetrate your heart and mind, constantly praying, 'Lord, speak to me.'
(3) When you first explore meditation, don't spend too long. A few minutes is probably enough — the time can be extended with experience.
(4) If you are with a group, meditate apart. Then gather together and encourage one another as you share ideas, and ask the Lord to speak to you through what the others have discovered.
(5) When you get home, note down some of the things which the Lord has spoken to you about. Make sure you follow them through in your everyday life.

Personal follow-up

After this initial experience of meditation, you may like to explore some of these other ideas.

Outdoors

(a) *The night sky filled with stars*

'You must shine among them like stars lighting up the sky, as you offer them the message of life' (Phil 2:15).

(b) *A stream babbling over pebbles*

'The water that I will give him will become in him a spring which will provide him with life-giving water and give him eternal life' (Jn 4:14).

(c) *Cliffs, sea and sky*

'Can anyone measure the ocean by handfuls or measure the sky with his hands? Can anyone hold the soil of the earth in a cup or weigh the mountains and hills on scales? Can anyone tell the Lord what to do?' (Is 40:12).

(d) *At sunrise*

'The Lord's unfailing love and mercy still continue, Fresh as the morning, as sure as the sunrise. The Lord is all I have, and so I put my hope in him' (Lam 3:22).

Indoors

Of course it is also possible to meditate indoors. It is important that there aren't too many distractions around in the room where we are to seek the Lord. Sometimes a symbol in the centre of the room can provide a focus for our thinking.

(a) *A loaf of bread*

'I am the bread of life, He who comes to me will never be hungry; he who believes in me will never be thirsty' (Jn 6:35).

(b) *A wooden cross*

'The greatest love a person can have for his friends is to give his life for them' (Jn 15:13).

As time goes by it will become possible to meditate without these visual aids. Just a verse from the Bible quietly repeated will be enough for you to meditate on.

Meditation is an important way of praying. In this noisy high-pressure society we'd all be a lot healthier in mind and spirit if we put in a few moments each day to seek the Lord sincerely and quietly.

2
Walking with the Lord

A long wait lay ahead of me at Venice airport. I checked in and passed through the security barrier, but when I reached the departure lounge I was told that the plane would be four hours late. I was unable either to move back out of the security barrier or forward to continue my journey.

I was trapped between countries, between cultures and between appointments. The departure lounge had an unreal atmosphere: hundreds of us were 'trapped in transit'. It was like being in 'no man's land'; life was in 'freeze frame'. Yet I found that this situation provided an ideal opportunity to draw close to the Lord. There was a transcendent quality about that night; time seemed to stand still.

A pilgrimage is somewhat similar. As we walk, we need to pause in the midst of life and learn what the great Christian mystics have described as 'practising the presence of Christ'. Sadly, many of us today have little or no experience of this discipline — and some of us have no desire to work at it.

In order to encourage one another to practise the presence of Christ, it's important that our pilgrimage is never hurried. There's no need to cover huge distances in miles.

Our aim is not to run a twenty-six mile marathon, but make a journey with the Lord which will enrich our lives. And we can only make such a journey leisurely. One way of stressing this would be to confiscate everyone's watch at the start.

As we make our pilgrimage, it's important that everyone understands that this isn't a race and that the fastest walkers must adopt the pace of the slowest person in the group. There must be plenty of time to pray and share along the way without anyone having to 'rush' or 'catch up'.

In this calm and unhurried mood we have the opportunity to focus on the 'author and finisher' of our faith, Jesus Christ. It is by thinking about him and by recognising his presence with us that we draw close to God. Jesus must always be the focus of our devotion, for he declared: 'I am the way, the truth and the life, no-one comes to the Father but by me.' He is the one who leads us to the Father, and so our attention must be on him.

My own relationship with Jesus has only developed after many years of searching. Although I knew about Jesus from the earliest days of my life, I didn't actually know him until I was a teenager.

When I was a few months old, my mother used to take me on her preaching engagements. Apparently, when I screamed she would rock my carrycot with her foot in the pulpit in the hope that I would go to sleep. I am deeply grateful for the Christian home in which I was brought up, for the daily prayers at my bedside, and for the encouragement to serve the Lord which my parents constantly gave. I knew more about the Bible and church life than any of my friends, but I was sometimes aware that I lacked a real depth of faith and a personal relationship with the Lord.

My own conversion was a story of struggle. I moved from a vague kind of belief in God to a living faith in Christ during my late teenage years. It was a period of much discussion, study and prayer.

First, I had to accept intellectually that Jesus existed as a real person. I read up on history and began to discover that there was evidence for Christ's life and ministry in the writings of early Jewish historians like Josephus.

I joined a teenage discussion group and although I started out as the argumentative sceptic in the group, I gradually became more and more convinced that Jesus was someone very special.

At school I was given a Gideon Bible, and I began to read the Gospel stories with a new interest and hunger. I discovered a ring of truth in them which fascinated me. I studied the epistles, and my faith was strengthened by the testimonies of people such as Peter, who wrote: 'We have not depended on made up legends in making known to you the mighty coming of our Lord Jesus Christ. With our own eyes we saw his greatness. We were there when he was given honour and glory by the Father' (1 Pet 1: 16–17).

I began to realise that Jesus was far more than just a 'nice guy'. The more I asked questions about him, read about him, and heard about him, the more I wanted to get to know him in a real way myself.

I came to see that no one throughout history could be compared to him; the affect of his life on individuals and on nations was immeasurable. And I was broken by the story of his love, for here was a man who not only preached forgiveness but hung on a cross to prove it.

My Christian friends convinced me to take Jesus seriously, and to search for him with all my heart. As I met more and more believers I began to want the kind of relationship with Jesus which they so obviously knew. I knew that my intellectual assent to Jesus was not enough because I hadn't really put my faith in him. Things came to a head one Easter weekend at a Christian youth camp where I heard a very elderly deaconness preach about the risen Jesus. On that Easter Sunday morning the story of the resurrection spoke to me in a new way.

After lunch I took time out from the rest of the group and went for a walk in the woods. When I was all alone in a thickly wooded area I knelt down and invited Jesus Christ into my life to be my friend and saviour. There was no dramatic experience, just a new sense of peace and of the closeness of Jesus. It was as though before my conversion Jesus was high on the mountaintops far away and I was down in the valley below. He was distant and unknowable, and even prayer was hopeless for he couldn't be reached. But when I came to know Jesus for myself he came down from the mountaintop and began to walk the valley by my side. He became my personal friend, and he was always there to share whatever joys or sorrows came my way.

My relationship with the Lord has matured over the years, and I find that I often draw closest to him as I walk alone. On occasions like this I often feel that Jesus is actually walking beside me. Silently I share my deepest needs with him, and sense his enfolding love around me.

When I went forward as a candidate for the Methodist ministry, the rather austere committee which interviewed me asked if I could define my 'experience of

Christ'. I shared my testimony and talked of the real relationship I shared with Jesus. I tried to explain that I was in Christ and he in me. I'm pleased to say that they accepted my rather hesitant explanation, and confessed that they wouldn't have liked to answer the question themselves.

It's not easy to define our experience of Christ, but Watchman Nee's simple explanation has always helped me to understand it better. Nee was once asked to explain his experience of Christ. He took a very hot cup of tea, dropped a lump of sugar into it, and stirred it well.

'Now,' he said to the young enquirer, 'try and take the sugar out of the tea!'

His young friend was exasperated! 'How can I? For the tea has become the sugar and the sugar has become the tea!'

'Exactly,' replied the great teacher. 'In the same way, I am in Christ and He is in me!'

Over the years, I have become part of Christ and he has become part of me as I have served him day by day. I have asked him to be the centre of all that I am and ever hope to be.

It's important to recognise that the Christian faith is a continual relationship with Jesus. One of the earliest pieces of advice I received as a young Christian was from Paul's letter to the Colossians.

> 'Since you have accepted Jesus Christ as Lord, live in union with Him. Keep your roots deep in Him, build your lives on Him, and become stronger in your faith . . .'

The secret of all Christian growth is maintaining this close union with the Lord. I have found that this intimate relationship with him is something which matures with the years. As time has gone by I have come to know him more fully, and to yield my life to him more completely. But I have never felt that I've 'arrived' in my relationship with the Lord — there is always more. TS Eliot's poem 'East Coker' sums up the fact that life is an ongoing pilgrimage into the love of the Lord.

> Old men ought to be explorers,
> Here and there does not matter,
> We must be still and still moving
> Into another intensity
> For a further union, a deeper communion . . . .

Just a few days ago I stood with a group of about ninety people in a field among the hills of Derbyshire. It was nearly midnight, in the clear night sky was a full moon bright enough to cast shadows around us. The sky was filled with millions of stars, and as we stood together a stillness descended upon us. We were soon standing in silent awe. The stars reached out into infinity, and the enormity of the universe dwarfed us.

As we stood there in the open field we prayed out loud. God was very close, and we seemed to be standing on the edge of eternity. Our breath steamed out into the chill night air as we sang in harmony 'Be still and know that I am God.' We knew that we were standing in the presence of one who was so much mightier and greater than we could ever imagine.

That night I caught a fresh glimpse of the Lord's majesty and power. I was facing major questions and decisions about my own future at the time, and it was good to regain my perspective on things as I stood before him. I knew that whatever I faced, the Lord would be with me. His presence was the foundation and security of my life.

As I stood in the presence of the living God that night, I was reminded of Jacob's experience at Bethel long ago. He was running away from home, and leaving behind all that was most precious and important to him. He felt alone, confused and afraid, for he was facing an unknown future. He used a stone for his pillow, and fell asleep. As he slept he saw a vision which has blessed countless millions of believers ever since. He saw the angels of heaven ascending and descending a ladder which stretched from earth to the very throne of God. In the dream the Lord assured him 'Remember, I will be with you and protect you wherever you go, and I will bring you back to this land . . .'

Jacob realised that the Lord was with him in the personal problems which were to him so insoluble, with him in the family conflicts and broken relationships, and with him in the confusing decisions which he didn't know how to make. From his high position in glory the Lord could see the way ahead so clearly. Many of us need to enter into the kind of exper ence of the Lord which Jacob had out there in the wilderness. We need a deeper sense of His presence in our everyday lives.

Jacob had sensed the presence of the Lord in a place that he didn't expect and in a way that blessed and encouraged him. After he awoke he took the stone that was under his head, poured olive oil over it, and dedicated it to God. He called the place *Bethel* which means 'house of God'. The stone was to be a reminder that even there in the wilderness the Lord was with him.

As we walk up many of the older tracks in the British countryside we come across piles of stones which mark the way. Many walkers throw a stone on to these 'cairns' as they pass by, and so the marker is perpetuated by each generation.

On our pilgrimage we will build our own cairn or marker to symbolise the Lord's presence with us, and to celebrate the fact that this place marks the location of a 'Bethel' or 'house of God'. Time and again in the Old Testament we read that anointing something or someone with oil is a symbol that they are 'set apart' or 'holy'. The pile of stones is as sacred as any cathedral, for it will be a 'house of God' for us. And so we will pour oil over it as a symbol that it marks a holy place. Here we will pause to remember the Lord's presence with us and we will offer simple prayers of praise and worship. As we stand by our cairn for a moment of silent prayer, we will claim the promise of Jesus 'I will be with you always.'

We would all find more peace, purpose and direction if we were to pause for a while each day and bathe in the radiance of his presence. We would all find more meaning to our lives if we could discover a 'Bethel' where we could experience Christ for ourselves.

In this uncertain and changing world, my experience of Christ is one of the few things that I know I can rely on in the years ahead. The fact that 'Jesus is the same yesterday, today and forever' is a sure foundation upon which to build my life.

Moses knew a lot about the assurance of the Lord's presence in all circumstances. When the people of Israel finally finished their great trek through the wilderness, they reached the banks of the River Jordan. They were at the threshold of the Promised Land. Yet Moses, who had led them through so many adventures in the wilderness years, knew that he would never enter the Promised Land. He summoned the leaders of the people to him and told them that Joshua would be their new leader. Because Moses knew that the people had come to depend on him for their security and strength, he gave them a final word of promise. 'Your God, the Lord himself, will be with you. He will not fail you or abandon you, so do not lose courage or be afraid.'

No matter what my future holds, I know that Jesus will be there to sustain and guide me. Whatever other changes I may face, I am assured that my relationship with him will remain sure and unshakeable. In the end, my friendship with Jesus is the most precious and lasting experience I can know.

It is now more than twenty years since I first asked Jesus into my life at the youth camp, but my experience of him has not dimmed in all that time. I look ahead to the future knowing that even in old age my relationship with Jesus will not disappoint me.

I have heard many testify that the experience of his love grows greater with the years. John Wesley, for example, preached his final sermon in Leatherhead at the age of 87 and then returned to his home in City Road, London. He knew that he had not long left to him on this earth, but over and over again during his last days of illness he repeated, 'The best of all is, God is with us!'

Even in death's dark hour John Wesley knew the Lord's sustaining presence to bless him and carry him through. We must bring this sense of Christ's presence to every situation we face. Jesus Christ stands ready to greet us as each new day dawns, and in this assurance we are able to press on into the unknown.

Wherever we go, the Lord is there. Whatever the future holds, he will give us grace to face it. But we must all maintain and nurture our relationship with him, for it is this friendship which is at the heart of all true Christian experience. If we want to deepen this relationship we must give it time, and in our everyday life we must learn how to 'practise the presence of Christ'.

The great Christian mystics down the centuries commend this practice as the essential starting-point for prayer.

At the end of the seventeenth century, Madam Guyon wrote one of the greatest classics on prayer: *Experiencing the depths of Jesus Christ*. It has enriched the prayer lives of countless millions of Christians down the years. She wrote:

> Dear child of God, all your concepts of what God is really like amount to nothing. Do not try to imagine what God is like. Instead, simply believe in His presence. Never try to imagine what God will do. There is no way God will ever fit into your concepts. What then shall you do? Seek to behold Jesus Christ by looking to Him in your inmost being, in your spirit.

If I had to share one piece of advice from my own experience of prayer it would be the importance of seeking Jesus. Too often in my own life I have rushed into his presence and gabbled my lists of praise points and intercessory needs. Over the years I have come to understand that I need to pause and wait in silence until I am prepared to meet with him.

The greatest requirement for those who would pray is a heartfelt desire to meet with Jesus and to share fellowship with him. Prayer is a developing relationship with Jesus; and we need to give time to it if we want to become mature Christian disciples.

Pilgrimage provides a good opportunity for learning how 'to practise the presence of Christ'. This is not something that can be 'taught', but rather a style of prayer that is 'caught' from others who walk the pilgrim way with us.

My favourite account of the resurrection is the walk to Emmaus. As the evening shadows lengthened two disciples met a stranger who walked beside them. They invited him to join them for supper, and as he broke the bread they recognised him — their risen Saviour.

Organising a church pilgrimage

Route 2: from the nature display to the cairn.

Aim: to encourage walkers to 'practise the presence of Christ'.

As the pilgrims leave the nature display, they are invited to talk about past experiences of the presence of God. Great care must be taken with those who are new Christians or who find it difficult to talk about their walk with the Lord. No pressure should be exerted on those who are reticent to speak. The leader and pastors circulate among the group, gently guiding the conversation and encouraging the pilgrims to answer questions like 'Have you ever known the presence of God?' 'What is it like to experience the Lord's presence?' 'How can we find a deeper sense of God's presence with us?'

When the group arrives at a suitable clearing or open space the leader asks everyone to go and find pebbles, rocks and boulders and to bring them back to the spot. As they go off looking for these stones each person is invited to 'Seek the Lord' and to know his presence in the quietness.

When they return the people in the group build their own pile of rocks to symbolise the Lord's presence with them, and to celebrate the fact that this place marks the location of a 'Bethel' or house of God. It would be good at this point if someone in the group could tell the story of Jacob in the wilderness.

The pilgrims pause to remember the Lord's presence with them in this holy place, and simple prayers of praise and worship are offered. Several of the group may ask the Lord to walk with them on this pilgrimage and to be present in every conversation and every activity.

The group then stands together for a moment of silent prayer, and each person claims the promise of Jesus 'I will be with you always.' Each one invites Jesus to be present with them on the journey, and pauses to 'practise the presence of Christ'.

As the pilgrims prepare to set off for their next marker, they each take a small pebble or stone with them as a permanent reminder that wherever they go the Lord will be there. Every place can be a 'Bethel' or a house of God for Jesus promised that He would never leave us nor forsake us.

On my son's window sill there is a strange assortment of bits and pieces which he's collected over many holidays. There's a piece of rock from the top of Snowdon, a reminder of his first 'climb'; there's a lovely piece of coral which came from some foreign holiday, and twigs which remind him of different walks in the forest.

This stone from the 'cairn' could be taken home by the pilgrims and put on display as a continuing symbol of the Lord's presence with us in all our tomorrows.

A sense of the Lord's presence should be an important part of our daily life as Christians. Jesus said 'Remain united to me, and I will remain united to you. A branch cannot bear fruit by itself; it can do so only if it remains in the vine. In the same way you cannot bear fruit unless you remain in me' (Jn 15:4).

If we give Jesus space in our lives he will come and stay with us for ever.

Organising a personal pilgrimage

'Practising the presence of Christ'

At the heart of Christian prayer is our relationship with Jesus Christ. Like all relationships we must work at it. The key to a deeper knowledge of the Lord is the discipline of 'practising the presence of Christ' which means talking with him in a real and personal way.

Preparation

We can only pray effectively if we have given our lives to Jesus and accepted his forgiveness and love. When we talk to him we shouldn't struggle and strain to understand him; we just need to welcome him to draw close to us. We claim his promise 'I will be with you always', and accept by faith that he is there.

Activity

Like Jacob of old we build a small 'Bethel' of stones and anoint it with oil. This reminds us that we are in a holy place, a house of God. Wherever we seek him he is there, so every place is holy. This cairn is just a symbol of his presence with us in this location.

Practical advice

(1) If we are going to meet with the Lord it may be good to 'make an appointment' to do so. Rather than drifting into prayer we may consider setting aside a specific time when we are going to meet with the Lord without interruption.
(2) Praise and worship are the preparation for meeting with Jesus. Many of the greatest prayers of the Bible begin with sections of praise and worship. As we lift high the name of Jesus and glorify him we provide a context in which we can share ourselves deeply with him. Praise is the doorway to meeting the Lord.
(3) It can be helpful to walk as we are praising and worshipping the Lord, but when we sense his presence with us we rest and are seated.
(4) As we seek Jesus in prayer we remember who he is and what he's done for us. We must always approach him with love, honour and respect. We can never repay him or deserve his love for us, we can only thank him and praise him for it.

(5) At the start of our prayer time we may use phrases such as 'Jesus, my Lord', 'Jesus, you died for me', and 'Jesus, King of the Universe' to set our hearts and minds in a right attitude to meet with him.

Personal follow-up

After the pilgrimage it would be good to continue to deepen and develop our relationship with Jesus Christ. The Lord is with us all the time and in every place, but we need to give all our attention to seeking him and meeting with him for at least a few moments every day.

It can be very helpful to read passages of Scripture which glorify and praise God as a preparation for 'practising the presence of God'. One of these passages can be read slowly, and then phrases from it can be repeated as we prepare to meet with the Lord.

Revelation 1:12–18 — A description of Jesus the King.

Psalm 103 — A meditation on the love of God.

John 10:1–18 — Jesus the Shepherd.

Many Christians find it helpful to meet with the Lord each day, and to have a regular place where they seek the Lord and share their lives with him.

3
Seed Faith

Many of us launch into our lives as new Christians with the kind of faith that can move mountains. Our prayers are alive and specific, and we look with eagerness to see how the Lord will answer them. Our faith matches the classic definition which is found in Hebrews 11:1 'To have faith is to be sure of the things we hope for, to be certain of the things we cannot see.'

But after a while church life can drag us down, and our simplicity of faith may disappear. Disillusionment slowly winds itself around our thinking, praying and planning and we become cold and half-hearted.

I have spotted this exhaustion and discouragement in many people who are involved in church life. I've met youth leaders who have slogged on year after year, and are now tired and fed up. Their initial enthusiasm has dwindled and the youth work has become a struggle.

Some ministers feel the same, for they often have to cope with entrenched attitudes and petty traditionalism. Sometimes the churches they pastor are facing overwhelming financial pressures or major building problems.

Such difficulties can cause their initial enthusiasm to evaporate and disillusionment to take root. I have met a few ministers who seem to be fed up with everything and everyone, and who find their work a great burden.

I understand how they feel because I went through a similar phase in my own ministry. After four years in theological college I entered the ministry with all the sensitivity of a bull in a china shop. I flew around trying to do everything myself, and hoping to change the church overnight. After a few months I was completely exhausted and somewhat discouraged.

When I was feeling particularly low in my first church an older and wiser minister came to see me. He told me that I was trying to do too much, too soon. He showed me that I had been setting targets for myself which were not the Lord's targets and that I'd been racing towards goals that he was not asking me to reach.

Some of us are trying to shoulder burdens which, in fact, we've not been asked to bear. The Lord has not called us to carry the mission of the church on our own because the work belongs to him and not to us. He will provide the resources to enable us to do his will.

When we're discouraged it's good to remember the great pioneers of the faith who have lived in other periods of history. We can gain great inspiration from their example because many of them knew worse times of opposition, disillusionment and hardship than we've ever seen and yet the Lord brought them through.

A pilgrimage can be a wonderful opportunity for walking in the footsteps of the great men and women of faith of previous generations. We can learn so much from them, and their lives can inspire us to greater service for the Lord in our generation.

One such pilgrimage begins on the Berkshire Downs and follows in the footsteps of Birinus, the great missionary of Wessex. The pilgrims pause by the River Thames during their journey to remember how Birinus baptised the Saxon king, an event which was a turning-point in the life of the church. As they pause at this spot the pilgrims can thank the Lord for the past and seek a fresh vision for the future.

Another popular pilgrimage, also designed to challenge people to serve the Lord, is organised by the Anglican diocese of Kent and is held every Easter Monday. Hundreds of people make a pilgrimage to Canterbury Cathedral in the footsteps of Augustine, the early Christian missionary whose monks evangelised England from AD 597.

A few weeks ago I joined this pilgrimage and at one point in the service, all the pilgrims were given candles. Gradually a flame was passed from candle to candle until they were all alight. We all lifted up our candles and sang the chorus 'Walk in the light'. I found it a poignant reminder that the light of Christ has been passed down to us from people like Augustine, and that the responsibility now rests with us to pass the gospel on.

There is a similar message behind the weekly pilgrimage around the tiny Scottish island of Iona. People from all over the world travel to visit this island to thank God for the work of an early Scottish missionary called Columba. He started with a dozen missionaries on Iona in AD 563 and from this base he planted churches all over Scotland. His mission influenced Scotland for many centuries and what began as something very small had far-reaching effects. Many people have been challenged by visiting the Christian community on Iona and by walking where Columba lived and worked. Some have found a fresh concern for mission and a new hope for the future of the church.

Pilgrimages such as these can bring us into a new awareness of the greatness of God and a fresh understanding of his purposes for our generation. They can offer a shaft of light which scatters doubt and stimulates us to trust him more.

This part of our pilgrimage is designed to help us focus on the mission of the church, and to gain a fresh sense of urgency to share our faith. At the completion of this third section of the pilgrimage we may discover a new sense of commitment to building the kingdom of God.

Pilgrimage has often been an opportunity for dreaming new dreams and seeing fresh visions, and as we pause to pray for the church the Lord may speak to us. It will all be worth while if just one youth leader discovers a fresh love for his group, or one minister sees new opportunities in his church, or one disillusioned church member catches a glimpse of what the church could be.

It would be helpful if this third stage of our pilgrimage could take place in the country. As we walk along we should look carefully at the trees, hedgerows and fields and absorb something of the beauty around us. The theme of our meditation is 'the mustard seed'.

One summer I went to help my friend bring in the harvest on his Yorkshire farm. I had no idea what harvesting would be like, and as I learnt how to drive the tractor, throw bales of straw into the barn and unclog the bailer, I began to realise just how stressful an occupation farming can be. Each night my friend Richard and I would stagger back into the farmhouse covered with sweat and grime, but with a glow of satisfaction that 'all was safely gathered in'.

One day we had to take a trailer of oil seed rape from

the combine harvester in the field to the large storage silo in the farmyard. I rode through the village on the back of this trailer piled high with shifting seed. I held on to the swaying trailer as we sped through the village but gradually I began to sink lower and lower until my wellingtons and trousers filled up with the rough black seed. It was not a pleasant experience.

When we arrived at the farmyard we lowered a large black suction pipe into the trailer and watched as the seed was sucked up into the silo. My friend sighed, and murmured, 'This stuff is amazing . . . we sow it in pounds, and reap it in tons!'

As I saw the crop gradually disappearing into the silo I remembered the parable of the mustard seed, and understood the full force of its meaning for the first time. There is growth potential in a grain of seed which is quite indescribable. Jesus said: 'The Kingdom of heaven is like this. A man takes a mustard seed and sows it in his field. It is the smallest of all seeds, but when it grows up, it is the biggest of all plants. It becomes a tree, so that the birds come and make their nests in its branches' (Mt 13:31–32).

This parable really came alive for me when I visited Gwennap Pit in Cornwall. Every year hundreds of Methodists travel to this large amphitheatre. It's the site where John Wesley used to preach to the Cornish tin miners in the open air, and where many hundreds found the Lord.

On one occasion when I visited Gwennap Pit an actor dressed as Wesley preached in the arena. It was a powerful reminder of Wesley's effective preaching ministry and of the way that the Lord used him to bring revival.

On that occasion there were young Methodists from

all over the world sitting in the amphitheatre. As I gazed around at that great crowd I was overwhelmed by the thought that the preaching of this one man could result in a worldwide church of over 50 million members. This was a powerful demonstration that the growth potential in any seed of the gospel is even greater than that of a grain of mustard seed!

Even though the route of our pilgrimage may not take us in the footsteps of someone like Wesley, Birinus or Augustine, we should still pause to remember the mission of the church and to consider our part in it.

In order to get people thinking about the mission of the church, every member of the group is given a handful of seed and asked to meditate on the parable of the mustard seed. During this meditation the group should glimpse the enormous 'growth potential' of the kingdom of God.

Few Christians seem to have much vision for growth potential in their local church. Wherever I go, I hear people talking about the difficulty of their particular 'patch' for the mission of the church. Those working in suburbia talk of apathy and materialism; those working in villages talk of traditionalism and the occult; and those working in the inner city talk of acute social need. Many Christians feel that it must be easier to witness for the Lord somewhere else.

In Christian ministry the grass may seem greener on the other side of the hill, but the fields over there are often just as barren. The history of mission demonstrates that the hardest ground can sometimes yield most fruit for the church, and that where Christians face really tough situations they discover what God can really do.

When Robert Raikes was a young man living in Gloucester he walked through the town square one

Sunday afternoon and saw the children playing there. They were illiterate, ill-disciplined and totally outside the life of the church.

Raikes despaired of the situation and felt that it was hopeless. Just then he heard a voice saying, 'Try, try, try!' He was so convinced that this was a divine commission that he started a Sunday school to help the children to read the Scriptures. Little did he know that a worldwide movement would grow from this small seed which would bring millions of children to a knowledge of Jesus Christ.

This rowdy group of children was hardly the best ground for such a movement to be sown in, but this was the group which the Lord chose. We should never turn our back on 'hard ground', because this might be just the place where Jesus wants us to work.

Having run youth groups in my home for over ten years, I've known quite a few bad moments. At some stage every group has had its problems, but one Sunday evening group was a particular pain. Sometimes I felt as if they were taking their teenage rebellion out on me rather than their parents.

My wife and I dreaded Sunday evenings, for every suggestion was opposed and every discussion-starter ridiculed. There were times when we felt like giving up the group altogether. It constantly baffled us that they kept coming even though they didn't appreciate what was on offer.

One of the most regular attenders at this group was a young black lad called Paul. Several years later I met him at a conference and I rejoiced that he had become a Christian and was a full-time youth worker in a Christian centre in the East End. He was a strong Christian, and was exercising a great ministry among these inner-city kids.

'By the way, Rob,' he whispered, 'did I ever thank you for running that youth group all those years ago? I don't know where I'd have been without it.'

I wouldn't have believed that such a harvest could have come from that difficult youth group, but there is greater growth potential in one grain of mustard seed than we can ever imagine.

Some of the group may like to sow the seeds they have been given in a patch of hard ground. It may be a piece of ground without much vegetation, or shaded from the sun, or perhaps with muddy soil.

By planting their seeds in such ground they can remember that the divine commission does not allow us to be 'choosy' in our seed-sowing. We are called to go into *all* the world, not just where the grass is greener.

In 1865 no one would have looked at the East End of London as a potential harvest for the kingdom of God. One night in that year, however, William Booth was walking home through the East End when he felt convicted by the needs of the people.

When he got home he told his wife, 'As I passed by the doors of those gin palaces tonight I seemed to hear a voice saying, "Where can you find such heathen as these, and where is there so great a need for your labours?" I felt as though I ought at all costs to stop and preach to those East End multitudes.'

William Booth was a popular preacher and successful evangelist, and he had a leadership role in the nationwide work of the Methodist church. Yet he turned his back on all this to respond to the needs of those whose lives were such a mess.

The seeds that William Booth sowed in the East End of London bore a harvest which was reaped throughout the world through the ministry of the Salvation Army. Who would have imagined that a movement of such fervour and compassion could have emerged from such a barren area.

When we plant the seeds of the gospel they have a growth potential which is beyond our understanding. As St Paul wrote, 'I sowed the seed, Apollos watered the plant, but it was God who made the plant grow. The one who sows and the one who waters really do not matter. It is God who matters, because He makes the plant grow' (1 Cor 3:6–7).

In one of my churches I was inundated with young couples who wanted to get married there. It had a very traditional interior, a tall spire and a garden for the photos, so it tended to attract couples for all the wrong reasons.

Each week I would hold 'wedding interviews'. I would often see three couples in an evening, spending an hour with each. During the months before the wedding I tried to give each couple three interviews in order to prepare them well.

The first meeting was very much a 'getting to know you' session, in which I established a relationship and discussed their plans. The final interview dealt with practical arrangements, and we would 'talk through' the service together. But the second interview was always the most crucial.

During this second talk I tried to convey the Christian teaching on marriage and something of how faith in Christ could strengthen and sustain their life together. I hoped that because of this conversation some of them might find the Lord at the start of their married life.

This second interview was always tricky. Sometimes the couple would steer the conversation away from anything spiritual, and throw in red herrings at every opportunity. I found some of these sessions very discouraging. It became obvious that some of these couples were just 'using the church' because they wanted a nice backdrop for their photos.

One couple, however, didn't try to steer the conversation away from the Lord, in fact they were anxious to know more. They came back again and again and eventually gave their lives to the Lord.

Last year I stood in their large Yorkshire manse and marvelled at what the Lord had done. Here they were, years later, about to start their own ministry. I fought back tears as I recalled the evening when they first came to enquire about their wedding, for now they witness to wedding couples themselves.

So there is enormous growth potential in every seed of the gospel which we sow, and some of those seeds will grow into tall trees.

Some members of the group may wish to spend time just looking at the tiny seed which they are holding and imagining the growth potential hidden within it. They could spend time preparing the soil for this seed by clearing undergrowth and using a twig to dig a furrow. For each seed we sow is precious and each one has the potential of harvest within it.

Sometimes the harvest may not be reaped for many years. Recently I met a young Indian Christian called Augustine. Some years ago he had a dream in which the Lord called him to give up everything and travel to northern India to plant churches. In simple obedience he sold his home, left his job and moved to northern India with his family.

He couldn't interest any missionary societies in his vision, but at last two elderly ladies working for the Elim

Church decided to support him. They had worked in the area for many years, and had found the people hard and unresponsive.

They offered hospitality to Augustine and his family and supported him in the early days of his ministry. Soon, however, their term of service was over and they returned home. It was a sad departure, because their combined work had shown no tangible results.

Augustine took on the work where they left off, and at last some very hardened criminals were converted to Christ. Such was the effect of these conversions on the local community that a church was formed. Augustine recruited others from the congregation to join him as missionaries, and soon there were congregations springing up in many villages around the area. There was still great opposition, but many came to know Christ.

I saw Augustine make an historic speech at the annual British Elim conference last year. He paid tribute to the faithfulness in prayer and witness of those two elderly missionaries, and declared that it was they who had sown the seed for the harvest he had reaped. At this conference meeting Augustine named a score of new churches 'Elim' in recognition of the seed-sowing ministry of these two British missionaries.

When we sow the seed of the gospel we may never know what harvest will one day be reaped. We are called to be faithful rather than successful. From time to time the Lord does give us a glimpse of the 'harvest', however, and it can come as a real surprise.

One night in Salford when I was 'on the road' with an evangelistic drama presentation called 'Travelling Workshop' my car was broken into and my case was stolen. I had to borrow clothes for the next stage of our journey, and I felt thoroughly fed up.

As we set out for Hull the next morning it was snowing heavily, and the M62 was like a skating rink. The thick snow piled onto the windscreen, and the engine laboured as we motored on through the deepening slush. My colleagues David Ash and Ruth Kellett had got streaming colds, so our journey was accompanied by the sound of much sneezing, wheezing and nose-blowing. As a team we were at an all-time low!

Eventually we found the church where we were to share our production, and a small audience of about thirty arrived and stamped their snowy feet all over the floor. In the corridor which was our dressing room we all groaned together. We'd gone all that way — and for what? Thirty people who were anxious to go home as soon as possible!

We cut the presentation short and returned to our digs feeling rather the worse for wear. There had been no response, and the whole enterprise had seemed a sheer waste of time.

Several years later, when I was speaking at a large student conference in Newcastle, a young woman came up to me and beamed.

'You won't recognize me but I gave my life to the Lord one night in a blizzard in Hull. Everything's been different since then, I never answered the appeal, but that was my night for commitment to Christ.'

We'd gone through a blizzard to sow some mustard seed, and there had, after all, been a harvest.

Since this time I have learnt that my most effective work is done when there has been a good foundation in prayer. I may sow the seed, but it is God who provides the harvest.

Much of our thinking in the church today focuses on what we can do, and what by our planning and efforts we can achieve. The history of the church demonstrates that where people have prayed and trusted God for great things, they have seen great results. All of us need to learn how to ask the Lord for great things. We need to discover again that 'To have faith is to be sure of the things we hope for, to be certain of the things we cannot see.'

Organising a church pilgrimage

Route three: from the cairn to the harvest-field

Aim: to encourage the pilgrims to pray for the mission of the church.

There is great joy in watching the life of nature all around us. As my family and I walked down an ancient track called Pilgrim's Way recently, we stopped to gaze spellbound as two wild rabbits hopped along before us.

As the pilgrims walk from the cairn towards the harvest-field, they could look at the signs of creation all around them. There may be those in the group who can put names to trees or flowers, or who can spot birds' nests or rabbits' warrens and explain things about the created world around us.

It would be good to talk together about the seasons, and the Lord's faithfulness in sending them. The death of winter is replaced by the new life of spring and the harvest of summer. The constant faithfulness of the Lord is demonstrated by the cycle of seed-time and harvest.

It would be helpful for the group to walk beside a harvest-field at this point, but any clearing or grassy patch could be used.

On a recent pilgrimage I took a group into a large field full of new green shoots of corn. We sat and talked together about the different references which Jesus made to seed-time and harvest. We thought about the 'seed growing silently', and the 'sower and the seed'. We discussed the harvest of the kingdom which is waiting to be reaped, and the urgency of gathering in the harvest. We recounted the story of waiting for the 'good seed' and 'bad seed' to grow before they were sorted. And then we remembered the powerful growth of the mustard seed.

The next activity on the pilgrimage is the sowing of seed. When everyone is settled and quiet, a handful of seed is distributed to each member of the group. As people pause to look at the seed, someone reads the parable of the mustard seed (Mt 13:31–32).

Each individual goes off alone to look at their seed, hear what the Lord is saying to them through this symbol, and to sow it wherever and however they wish (though not near a field bearing crops!).

One person may choose a piece of 'hard ground' for their seed, and set about planting it carefully. They may like to pray for some aspect of their witness which they find very difficult or for some part of the church's work which seems very barren.

Another may like to throw their seed to the wind, remembering that the harvest is the Lord's responsibility and not ours. In doing this they may pray for their own witness, that what they say and do might influence those all around.

As others prepare the ground and plant the seed in good soil, they may like to pray that specific people for whom they have a special burden might find the Lord.

This simple act is often very powerful, and God seems to say different things to people through it. One person may be challenged to witness more faithfully at work, another might find a fresh commitment to children's work or youth outreach, and someone else may glimpse new hope for their local church.

After each person has sown their seed, they spend some moments praying for the mission of the church in the world, and for their particular part of the church's mission.

The leader should remind the group of the importance of praying for the mission of the church. It is only when a church is mobilised in prayer that it begins to see the seeds it sows grow to harvest.

Organising a personal pilgrimage

Prayer for revival

The church has made many schemes for renewal and growth, but recently there has been a new commitment to prayer for revival. As members of the church of Christ we need to recognise again that no matter how well we cultivate the soil or how widespread we sow the seed that only God can provide the harvest. As individuals and as churches we need to rediscover the importance of praying regularly for the renewal of the church and revival in our land.

Preparation

It would be good to read some of the following verses as a preparation to prayer for revival.

> 'I tell you the truth, if you have faith as small as a mustard seed, you can say to this mountain, "Move from here to there" and it will move. Nothing will be impossible for you' (Mt 17:20–21)

> 'Have faith in God,' Jesus answered. 'I tell you the truth, if anyone says to this mountain, "Go, throw yourself into the sea," and does not doubt in his heart but believes that what he says will happen, it will be done for him. Therefore I tell you, whatever you ask for in prayer, believe that you have received it, and it will be yours' (Mk 11:22–24)

> The apostles said to the Lord, 'Lord, increase our faith.' He replied, 'If you have faith as small as a mustard seed, you can say to this mulberry tree, "Be uprooted and planted in the sea," and it will obey you.' (Lk 17:5–6)

> 'Before they call I will answer; while they are still speaking I will hear.' (Is 65:24)

Activity

We take some seeds and decide where to plant them. As we plant these seeds we remember the seed of God's kingdom which has such growth potential. As we plant each seed we pray for one of our friends, and believe God for a great 'harvest' in this situation.

Personal follow-up

Identify two or three non-believers within your own circle of friends who you will pray for regularly over the coming months. Write down their names, and commit yourself to care for them and serve them as well as pray for them.

Widen your vision. Attend larger events and conferences where Christians gather to pray for revival in a country, continent or throughout the world. Thousands of Christians are doing this regularly, and every great revival can be traced back to movements such as these.

Begin to read the accounts of some of the great Christian revivals of history, and see what a prominent part prayer played in each of them.

Keep a record of those you pray for over the years and how the Lord has blessed, guided and kept them.

Read the Acts of the Apostles and note how important prayer was to the ongoing mission of the church. Look at ways of deepening the prayer life of your local church or house-group.

Practical advice

(1) Pray daily for these friends on your prayer list; and ensure that your love for them is genuine and sincere.
(2) Meet with other Christians and pray through each other's lists, sharing how the Lord has been answering your prayers.
(3) Encourage your church to start a regular prayer meeting to pray for those outside the church, and support the mission of the church with committed prayer.
(4) Don't be discouraged if your prayers aren't answered quickly. Sometimes we need to spend years in prayer before we see the harvest in someone's life.
(5) Remember that however difficult or fruitless your own service for the Lord may seem, it is God who

provides the harvest. Keep pressing on, remembering that the harvest will come even if we don't see it this side of eternity. We are called to remain obedient and faithful.

4
The Wilderness Experience

Most of us have known at least one or two hard times in the Christian life. Times when the cost of discipleship has seemed too great, or the struggle against temptation too difficult. In such 'wilderness experiences' it can be a great strength to remember those who have come through similar problems by trusting the Lord.

We can also find strength and inspiration from those who have been persecuted for their faith. Down the years many people have been willing to give their lives so that the gospel might be preached, the Bible printed or the right of worship established. Many of the things which Christians take for granted have been won by the suffering and bloodshed of the martyrs.

The stories of the martyrs have given strength and inspiration to many former generations of Christians, but few of us today know much about them. This is an aspect of Christian heritage which has been undervalued in recent years and pilgrimage gives us an opportunity to rediscover it.

Since the earliest days of the church there have

been pilgrimages to the graves of Christian martyrs. Some of the first pilgrimages were in memory of a martyr called Polycarp, who died in AD 155. Every year Christians would meet where he was killed to offer thanks to God for his commitment to Christ and to give their own lives back to the Lord.

In Rome pilgrims visited shrines dedicated to St Peter and to St Paul, and paused to pray near their bones. At Santiago de Compostela in Spain thousands of pilgrims gathered where St James had been laid to rest. Such pilgrimages were often powerful times of rededication.

Unfortunately the shrines quickly lost their spiritual significance and the church used them as a way of raising money for new buildings. Many unhelpful traditions grew up around the 'shrines of the martyrs'; and some of them came to resemble circus sideshows. Superstition flourished, and many pilgrims believed that the relics of the saints could impart mystic powers.

Canterbury was an example of how something very meaningful quickly deteriorated into a ghoulish side-show. The Canterbury pilgrimage originated with the murder of Archbishop Thomas Beckitt in the cathedral in 1170. The cathedral was cloed for twelve months and then it reopened as a place of pilgrimage.

Tens of thousands of people from all over the world made pilgrimages to Canterbury out of respect for Thomas. But a pilgrimage to the cathedral wasn't just an opportunity to pause in thanksgiving, it was an opportunity to see:

> The whole arms of eleven saints; part of the arm of St Jerome and a piece of the arm of St Paulinius, the bed of the blessed virgin Mary and wool of her own weaving; a fragment of the rock on which the cross stood, a piece of rock

from the Holy Sepulchre, others from the manger, the column at which our Lord was scourged and the stone on which He stood before His Ascension, Aaron's rod, and a piece of the clay from which Adam was made.[1]

In areas where the church could not find a suitable martyr to 'enshrine' there was pressure to find other suitable candidates. These were called 'confessors' – people who had faithfully 'confessed' the faith during their lives.

Unfortunately there wasn't an effective way of administering this 'confessor' system, and these shrines sprang up everywhere. Any church could construct a shrine if the people wanted one. The motives behind their construction were often dubious, and some of the 'confessors' were not all that they should have been.

Obviously we want to avoid these excesses on our own pilgrimage, and my own free church background makes me very suspicious of any hint of giving the 'worship due to God to men and women', or of building shrines. Yet I do believe that there is room in contemporary church life to pause and remember with thanksgiving those whose lives have been an outstanding testimony to the Lord.

This is the 'now' generation and the important time-frame is the present. Many contemporary Christians seem to be uninterested in the past. I believe that a glance backwards would help many of us to rediscover our 'roots' as Christians, and to learn something more about the faith of those who've gone before.

I experienced this for myself when I visited a Kenyan village some years ago. One steaming hot afternoon I joined hundreds of villagers as they marched along a country track to visit the graves of early missionaries. There was an intensity of feeling among the people in that procession and in the worship which followed. I discovered later that their ancestors had murdered those missionaries.

That annual pilgrimage reminded those villagers of their history. They remembered the cost which those early missionaries had paid, and they thanked God for them. But it wasn't only a time for looking back, it was a time of thanksgiving for the gospel itself and an opportunity for each villager to rededicate his life to the Lord.

Few of us in Britain have ever shared in an experience like this, or taken time out to discover the cost which many of our Christian forefathers have paid so that we might know the gospel. There is something very meaningful about visiting places where people have lived or died for Jesus.

Every year many Christians make a pilgrimage to the West Country village of Tolpuddle to recall the enormous price which those people paid for their commitment to the Lord.

The people of Tolpuddle were badly treated by their employers. Their wages went up and down at the whim of their overseers, and many of them were on the brink of starvation. They refused to accept their pay and banded together as a Christian fellowship against those who devalued their labour.

They saw their cause as an integral part of their Christian discipleship. Their stand brought them into dispute with the local authorities and eventually they were deported to Australia where they faced great hardship.

This annual procession at Tolpuddle is an important reminder that there is a price to pay in standing up for justice and righteousness. The Tolpuddle martyrs were willing to pay that price, and those who walk in their footsteps must ask what price we are called to pay in our generation.

Our pilgrimage may not take us along such an historic trail, but we can still make space to remember the lives of those whose quality of faith and commitment can be a challenge to our own today. We should never forget that we follow in the footsteps of many great disciples along the pilgrim road, and that the difficulties they encountered on their journey can be an inspiration to us as we walk 'through the wilderness'.

To illustrate this, it would be helpful if this section of the pilgrimage was the most difficult part of the walk! An area of rough scrubland, or a path that was difficult or steep, or an overgrown area where progress was slow would all help to highlight the theme of 'wilderness'.

The Christian life is sometimes a 'wilderness experience' and as the walkers are going along this part of the track they may like to think quietly about experiences of wilderness they have known. It's best if this wilderness section is walked alone, because experiences of 'wilderness' often make us feel lonely and isolated.

I recently took my family on a Saturday hike along Pilgrim's Way near our home in Surrey. The path started off all right, but we quickly discovered that we had chosen a very difficult section of the route.

What began as a gentle afternoon stroll became a steep hill climb, and after an hour we stopped in a clearing, breathless and worn out. From this vantage point we could see clearly that we had a lot more climbing to do. The view was spectacular, but we wondered whether to press on or turn back.

Walking up that steep track was not easy. We made slow progress, and did not feel we were covering the ground quickly enough. It was a step-by-step walk and we looked forward to easier times ahead.

The society in which we live is like a 'wilderness' to many Christians. Those of us who are totally committed to the Lord in Britain are in the minority, and we face all kinds of pressures as we serve Christ and live lives worthy of his disciples. There are times when being a committed Christian is rather like walking up a steep hill, with the path narrow and difficult.

The path of Christian discipleship can be hard — whatever your age. A survey of nine-year-olds revealed that most of them viewed Jesus Christ in the same way as they did Father Christmas. They said that belief in Jesus was just 'for the young kids'. I found the survey hard to believe until my son's teacher asked the class 'Who believes in Jesus?' My nine-year-old son was the only one to raise his hand.

Our secular society can often feel like a 'wilderness' to those who serve the Lord. One girl in my youth group was humiliated by her science teacher because she stood up for Christ. Her teacher made her defend her faith in front of the whole class and no one was willing to stand up and support her.

I went through a similar experience when I attended a secular training course some years ago. One of the trendy things to do at that time was to experience a 'T' group, which involved being analysed by eight others. We were shut up together in a suburban lounge for six hours, and there was 'full and frank' conversation.

Eventually they turned their attention to my faith, and I found myself ridiculed for my commitment to Christ and considered naive because of my moral stand on various issues. I found the experience very unnerving and I felt quite hurt. It was a time 'in the wilderness' for me.

It's only when you make a stand for Christ that you begin to taste the wilderness experience. You can be a Christian at work for twenty years without any hassle if you keep yourself to yourself. But if you ever 'go public' about your faith, you can become the butt of much joking and scorn.

Make a stand on some ethical issue, refuse to work on Sundays, say no to back-handers or always tell the truth . . . and you'll soon begin to walk the wilderness path. Read your Bible on the train, speak about Jesus in an open-air meeting, or invite your friends to an evangelistic meeting — and you'll sense just how much you stand out from the crowd.

Paul knew the pain of this kind of antagonism. In Corinth he worked among the Jewish community and testified that Jesus was the Messiah. But 'they opposed him and said evil things about him' (Acts 18:6). It was a painful experience to be rejected by his own people — he knew the wilderness all right.

In this wilderness experience when he felt so isolated he had a beautiful vision of Jesus. The Lord said, 'Do not be afraid, but keep on speaking and do not give up, for I am with you.' When it felt as though everyone else had rejected him, Paul knew that Jesus had not left him. Even in the wilderness, the Lord was there.

As we walk along the wilderness section of our pilgrimage it is good to reflect on wilderness situations we have known in our lives, and to remember that even at times like these the Lord has been with us.

The wilderness through which Jesus walked during the forty days and nights of his temptation was a dry and unpleasant place; but in all the temptations he faced he did not give in. There was a wilderness all around him, but no barrenness in his soul. He was never out of touch with his heavenly Father.

We may have to walk through a wilderness but it doesn't mean that our lives become barren. Some of the greatest Christian ministries have been exercised in the most hopeless situations, and many of the greatest Christian lives have been lived in the context of great personal suffering.

In every wilderness experience, 'Let us keep our eyes fixed on Jesus, on whom our faith depends from beginning to end. He did not give up because of the cross! . . . Think of what he went through; how he put up with so much hatred from sinners! So do not let yourselves become discouraged and give up' (Heb 12:2–3).

Most of us have known difficulties at home or at work and have walked through times of wilderness. But there's another kind of wilderness, too — a wilderness 'within' when God seems far away and we find it hard to pray.

A couple of years ago I visited about a dozen 'lapsed' members of a large suburban church. As most of them were London commuters the only time when I could catch them at home was late in the evening. I made an appointment with each one and managed to visit them all.

I was dreading those visits because I expected a hostile reception, but I needn't have worried because every time I was warmly received and found them eager to share.

None of them could explain why they had stopped attending church, for they had never made a conscious decision to quit. The transition from 'active' to 'lapsed' had not been a sudden one. There had been a seeping away of faith, a gentle decline in spirituality, and a gradual cooling of their relationship with the Lord.

Many of them talked freely about how their faith had waned and how their relationship with the Lord had grown weak. A couple of them actually admitted that they had grown more interested in the things of the world than the things of the Spirit.

I only wish that they had taken to heart Paul's advice to the Romans: 'Do not conform yourselves to the standards of this world, but let God transform you inwardly by a complete change of your mind' (Rom 12:2). They had allowed the 'wilderness' of the world to create a wilderness within.

But others confessed that when the going had got hard in the Christian life, they had given in and lost their hold on Jesus. I often find that those who fall away as Christians lack stickability. When things have grown tough in their relationship with the Lord they have quickly given up. They have been unable to 'keep on keeping on' when the road ahead has been steep and hard.

Recently I went on a hike with my two sons around a nature reserve in Kent. The first hour was a great success, and we made good progress. But it was a hot sticky day, and both my sons got quickly tired, and as the afternoon wore on we all felt like giving in.

Both my sons wanted to take the short-cut back to the start of the nature trail. But we 'kept on keeping on' and discovered many wonderful things in the nature reserve which would have been hidden from us if we'd turned back too soon. As we completed the trail and looked back across the track we'd travelled, I saw clearly that we had made progress by slowly plodding on, one step at a time.

In my own Christian life I have discovered that a similar principle applies and I call it 'the Christian plod'.

Regrettably I spend much of my time counselling people who are suffering spiritual 'lows' or looking for spiritual 'highs' in the Christian life. I try to encourage them to maintain the Christian plod!

When I've been in the wilderness myself, I've discovered that I've made most progress by 'keeping on keeping on' in my plod with the Lord. It is in this disciplined plod that I rediscover the Lord's blessing and a new anointing on my ministry.

Many Christians who are experiencing a 'wilderness of the soul' are looking for spiritual pick-me-ups. When they don't find them they become disillusioned and give up — they are not willing to maintain the Christian plod.

At this point in our pilgrimage, the group might like to pray for any among them who are facing specific problems at that time, that they may be sustained in the wilderness and guided in the days ahead.

The pilgrims share together something of the importance of the Christian plod when we are going through experiences of wilderness, remembering how vital it is to maintain a daily discipline of prayer, and to continue with it no matter how we feel spiritually. Members of the group could share ideas on how and when they pray.

It is in the plod of Christian fellowship, the plod of a disciplined prayer time, the plod of attendance at worship, and the plod of Christian commitment that we find the blessing that we once knew.

The Christian plod may not seem very exciting, but I believe it is the surest way out of the wilderness within. For as we continue to seek the Lord in prayer through thick and thin, we will find the renewal and guidance we need.

Prayer is the way out of the wilderness within, and the less we feel like prayer the more important it is that we pray. It is in the hard graft of prayer, the discipline of prayer and the plod of prayer that the Lord breaks in and takes us closer to him.

The Christian life rests on facts, not feelings. No matter how flat or dry we may feel, it is still important to pray and to seek the Lord. Perhaps at times like this it's even more important.

On our pilgrimage we spend some moments alone. We move to a place somewhere along the wilderness trail, and find some fallen twigs. Kneeling in the trail we make the letters of our initials with the twigs and lay them prominently along the path.

These initials on the trail are a symbol that we are laying our lives down for the Lord, and no matter how hard the journey may seem we are willing to pay the price. As we lay down our initials we commit our lives silently to the Lord, offering to him our experiences of wilderness and committing ourselves to follow him.

On the recent walk with my two sons we took a wrong turn. I don't know how it happened because the nature trail we'd been following was clearly signposted and the pathway easy to follow.

We must have been distracted and turned right instead of left — my navigation skills are not good at the best of times! Before long we were completely lost, and that awful sinking feeling flooded over us — should we press on or turn back? My sons looked at me in desperation — they had been with me in this situation before.

We decided to press on but the path got narrower and narrower until I had to carry my youngest son through a bed of stinging nettles. It was obvious that we had left the 'beaten track' and had turned off into the wilderness.

As we live the Christian life it's good to remember that we're not called to walk through a wilderness but to follow a well-beaten track. Countless millions of believers all around the world have gone on before us, and their experience can be an inspiration and blessing to us as we follow on behind. Their lives have blazed a trail for us, and their testimony provides a marker for us to follow. Silvester Horne's old hymn sums this up so well:

> For the might of thine arm we bless thee, our God, our fathers' God;
> Thou hast kept thy pilgrim people by the strength of thy staff and rod;
> Thou hast called us to the journey which faithless feet ne'er trod;
> For the might of thine arm we bless thee, our God, our fathers' God.
>
> May the shadow of thy presence around our camp be spread;
> Baptize us with the courage thou gavest to our dead;
> O keep us in the pathway their saintly feet have trod;
> For the might of thine arm we bless thee, our God, our fathers' God.

When I was in the Scouts we used to take great delight in 'tracking'. I well remember setting off along a maze of paths and trying to follow the trail which others from our troop had carefully laid. As the hours passed by we became more and more adept at spotting the track and following its direction. Where at first we had spent a long time searching for each marker we soon began to find them straight away.

In times of personal wilderness it's good to remember those who've laid down markers for us across the years and to thank the Lord for them. Church history describes countless people of conviction like Luther, of faith like

Wesley, of conscience like Wilberforce, and of zeal like Booth. Many of them faced greater difficulties and wilderness experiences than we'll ever know, and yet they overcame them with a quality of victorious hope which we need today.

Many of us are called to make our pilgrimage through difficult terrain. But the struggle of the pilgrim is nothing new, and we would all gain much by understanding more of those who've followed the same path in previous generations.

As I look back across my life I'm aware that today I am following a pathway which Christians I have loved have laid down for me to follow. From the earliest days of my childhood my parents taught me about Jesus and guided me in my thinking, and I am forever grateful to them for that.

Across the years there have been countless folk, many of whom I can't even remember or put a name to, who have guided me and whose lives have helped to show me the way ahead.

Recently I was preaching in a large church in the Potteries. Going back was quite an emotional experience because I had grown up there as a child. I hardly recognised the place because the main sanctuary had been rebuilt and the other premises completely modernised.

When I entered the old Sunday-school building I spotted a long curved bannister and immediately the memories of my Sunday-school days were unlocked. That was the bannister which I used to slide down when I was about six-years old!

The bannister triggered memories of my Sunday-school teacher, and how on Sunday afternoons she took us home for tea. I don't remember much about her lessons, but I still remember the cakes! In a very real way the pilgrimage of that dear soul who died so long ago is part of my pilgrimage, and I'm still a part of hers. As I look back across my life I am aware of many such unsung heroes whose ministry has guided me in the way.

When things are tough, and we are facing the many pressures which the world puts upon us it's good to remember that we are just a part of the great pilgrim train that cannot be numbered. This procession stretches down the centuries before us, all the way back to our leader, the Lord Jesus Christ.

It's also important to recognise that our witness in this generation will become a marker for others to follow. For behind us, yet unborn, are countless new believers following on.

Organising a church pilgrimage

Route four: from the wheat field through the wilderness.

Aim: to teach the discipline of prayer and the cost of discipleship.

At the start of this wilderness section, the guide gathers the group of pilgrims together and invites them to think about the times of wilderness which they have known in their lives.

These wilderness experiences might be external and relate to times when they have felt isolated as Christians. Or they may be internal and relate to what the Christian mystics have described as 'the dark night of the soul' when the Lord has seemed far away.

They walk over the wilderness section in silence, and after completing the major part of the section, gather together to share their 'wilderness experiences'.

The pilgrim guide explains to the group something of the importance of the Christian plod in experiences of wilderness. The guide stresses how vital it is to maintain a daily discipline of prayer, and to continue with it no matter how we feel spiritually.

Each member of the group is invited to spend some moments alone. This is an opportunity to commit themselves afresh to the Lord. No matter what 'personal wilderness' we may face, it is surely the life of prayer that will see us through.

As a symbol of this commitment to a daily discipline of prayer, each member of the group gathers a few twigs and pieces of grass and marks their initials in the track.

These initials are a reminder that 'people of prayer' have passed this way, and that these lives have pointed the way for many others to follow. Even in the wilderness our lives can be a witness and strength to others, and even in the wilderness there is power in prayer.

Organising a personal pilgrimage

The prayer of commitment

At the end of evangelistic missions we are sometimes invited to offer a prayer of commitment. This can be a very meaningful thing to do. But the prayer of commitment shouldn't only be used on such occasions; we should be offering prayers of commitment every day of our lives, especially in times of 'wilderness'.

Preparation

Read some passages of Scripture which challenge us to commitment:

> How hard it is for rich people to enter the Kingdom of God! It is much harder for a rich person to enter the Kingdom of God than for a camel to go through the eye of a needle. (Lk 18:24).
>
> I assure you that anyone who leaves home or wife or brothers or parents or children for the sake of the Kingdom of God will receive much more in this present age and eternal life in the age to come. (Lk 18:29).
>
> There is a large harvest, but few workers to gather it in. Pray to the owner of the harvest that he will send out workers to gather in his harvest. Go! I am sending you like lambs among wolves (Lk 10:3).
>
> Anyone who starts to plough and then keeps looking back is of no use to the Kingdom of God (Lk 9:62).
>
> If anyone wants to come with me, he must forget self, take up his cross every day, and follow me. For whoever wants to

save his own life will lose it, but whoever loses his life for my sake will save it (Lk 9:23).

Activity

We gather twigs and pieces of grass and mark out our initials on the wilderness path as a symbol of our lives laid down for Jesus.

Practical advice

(1) Before we commit our lives afresh to the Lord, it can be helpful to pause for a few moments to remember the cross, and to consider the sacrifice which Jesus made for us there.

(2) Many Christians offer themselves back to the Lord at the start of each new day and this can put the activities of the whole day in the right context. One Christian I knew used to commit himself to the Lord at his office before starting work.

(3) Some people find it helpful to kneel or lie prostrate when offering their lives to the Lord; but it is even more vital to prostrate our minds and hearts before him in commitment.

(4) It's important that we offer ourselves to be used in whatever way the Lord wishes. This may involve us dedicating ourselves to him in situations where we must be willing to take the humbler role.

(5) We offer our possessions and recognise that he has first call on our money, car and home; and in giving our time we recognise that it's a gift from him. We must also offer our talents so that he can really use us in his service.

Personal follow-up

Do an annual 'stock-take' on your life looking at what you've given and what you've still held back. An ideal time for this would be on a birthday or at the start of a new year.

Read and learn these words from the Methodist Covenant service and apply them to the different areas of your life.

The Covenant Prayer

I am no longer my own, but yours;
Put me to what you will,
Rank me with whom you will;
Put me to doing,
Put me to suffering;
Let me be employed for you,
Or laid aside for you;
Exalted for you,
Or brought low for you;
Let me be full,
Let me be empty;
Let me have all things,
let me have nothing;
I freely and wholeheartedly yield all things to your pleasure and disposal.

Notes

1 Alan Kendall, *Medieval Pilgrims* (Wayland: Hove, 1970).

5
A View of the World

Many recent pilgrimages have drawn attention to major public issues. One of my friends went on a pilgrimage to the Greenham Common missile base. When the group arrived it was surrounded by the police. The whole incident was quite unnerving.

Prayer at a location which highlights an issue can help to focus the mind and make our intercessions specific and meaningful. In places like Greenham Common, a pilgrimage can have the power of a prophetic symbol and involve us in political action.

Recently I served on the Council of Reference for 'March For Jesus' and caught something of the vision for that prayer pilgrimage. The vast procession numbering tens of thousands of pilgrims marched through the centre of London and prayed for aspects of the City's life such as the work of Parliament, the Stock Exchange and the BBC.

This pilgrimage was an important reminder that we should pray for these influential agencies in society and ask the Lord to guide those who control them. We must understand that intercession is vital and that we have a responsibility to pray regularly for the world.

Pilgrimages which have a strong social content give us a heightened awareness of the world's needs, and a recognition of God's involvement in all things. Pilgrimage is not an escape from reality, but an opportunity to face up to the needs of the world.

The brothers from the monastic community of Taizé in France have organised many pilgrimages to pray for the world. These pilgrimages often have a strong prophetic edge to them and pilgrims from all over the world get involved.

During their visit to London several years ago, the Taizé pilgrims divided into groups to pray for the city. I remember one group visiting an area where there was great racial tension. I found it deeply moving to see them praying around the area in the pouring rain.

Many of these pilgrims had travelled hundreds of miles, and although they prayed in a multiplicity of languages they knew the unity of the Spirit. Their presence in the area was a poignant symbol of the power of Christ to unite people of many different cultures.

Our pilgrimage may not take us to the site of a nuclear missile base or other 'sensitive' areas, but we should still take time to pray for the needs of the world. This section of our pilgrimage is called 'A view of the world', and if possible should take the group on a path with a good view of a town or village.

There is something very special about looking down on a town or village. The houses seem so small and the cars and people so insignificant. A view over a town can help us to put everything in perspective. Thousands of years ago Isaiah glimpsed the Lord's 'view of the world' and he wrote:

Do you not know? Were you not told long ago? Have you not heard how the world began? It was made by the one who sits on his throne above the earth and beyond the sky; the people below look as tiny as ants (Is 40:21–22).

Recently I took a committee up the Great Orme, a steep mountain above Llandudno. We walked along a path overlooking the town, and spent some time praying over the area. It was a very meaningful experience, and all of us gained a new sense of the Lord's all-embracing love for that community.

As we stop to look over a view of a town we should try to look at the world from the Lord's perspective. The Lord sees beyond the neatly ordered streets and into the suffering of human hearts. As we look at the world through the Lord's eyes we must ask him to give us a new vision of those in need.

None of us can cope with the suffering of the whole world, nor can we respond to all the needs around us. But we all have a God-given commission to care for those in need, and we have no excuse for neglecting those who cry for help. As we pause on our walk and look down at the view before us, we need to ask the Lord for a fresh understanding of the suffering in the world.

Before we can pray for a need we have to identify it. In our 'view of the world' we need to glimpse the pain that lies behind the doors of the community before us. We need to understand the pain of broken relationships, crushing bereavement, disabling illness and desperate loneliness which overshadows every city.

Several years ago I saw the needs of the people around me in a completely new way. I started writing a devotional column for a small free newspaper in our area. This free sheet had just been introduced by a young journalist working from a back-street shop in South London.

At that time the concept of a free newspaper was still fairly new, and the paper really caught on quickly. Before I knew it, my little devotional column had developed into a Christian counselling and care service sponsored by the Manpower Services Commission. We had a paid part-time staff of ten and a weekly circulation exceeding 100,000 homes. Gradually we built up a case-load of 3,500 clients.

This project opened up a new world of human need to me. I'd been a church minister for nearly ten years but I'd no concept of the suffering all around me. I'd driven around my 'parish' and visited church members, but I'd remained blindly unaware of the social problems which lay down every street.

The calls which came into the Helpline showed the great need for bereavement counselling. It became obvious that many people needed more than a short crematorium service and a business like call from the vicar; they cried out for long-term care and support.

I met the parents of cot-death babies whose grief was indescribable and who desperately needed support. Their friends had made light of their grief, saying, 'After all, it was only a baby, you can always have another.'

At our weekly case conference we came across countless situations where people had 'fallen through the net' of the caring services. Our counsellors found themselves trying to offer Christian compassion to those facing problems like homelessness, domestic violence, acute depression and crippling illness.

I was astonished to discover that many homeless families were living in bed-and-breakfast accommodation in our area — with all the attendant pressure that this put on family life. We did our best to agitate for more accommodation, but we only scratched the surface of a huge problem.

Unfortunately we found it very difficult to communicate these needs to the local churches. It sometimes felt as though Christians could respond to needs overseas more easily than the suffering in the streets nearby. The truth is that it can be more costly to care for the people next door than those you never meet, and sometimes getting involved with people can be harder than giving money to charity.

The local volunteer bureau appealed to us to provide support for the elderly within the community. Would anyone visit an elderly blind lady who sat at home all day and never had a visitor? Would anyone support local occupational therapists with essential follow-up work among the handicapped? Would anyone with a car take an eighty-year-old to visit his wife in hospital? Finding suitable volunteers was nearly impossible.

I had lived in a densely populated community, attended a lively and closely knit church, and yet gone about the area blithely unaware of the suffering which lay behind the doors of every street. Through the Helpline I began to discover that many people are fighting for survival in a society that doesn't much care.

We need to lift our eyes above our own problems and see the dark shadow of suffering on every side. As we pause to look down on our 'view of the world' we ask the Lord to help us comprehend the pain which floods throughout our area.

Sometimes it's good to base a whole pilgrimage around the needs within our area. The people of Notting Hill Methodist Church didn't go to some pretty woodland area for their pilgrimage. They just walked the streets around their church and focused on the needs they saw all around them. They read the stories of Jesus at various locations in their neighbourhood. In a community which has known times of intense racial tension and social deprivation this project demonstrated that the teaching of Jesus was not 'pie in the sky' but directly relevant to the needs of the area.

As we pause to look at our 'view of the world', the streets and houses become a symbol of all communities around the world. We think of places like Soweto, Beirut, Peking or Belfast, but we also picture the streets of our own town and remember the suffering there.

We must begin to understand that people with problems are crying out for someone to listen, and they are using the national Helplines to register their cry for help. The statistical review *Social Trends*, which was published by the government in 1984, reveals just how vast this need is.

Al-anon, which supports the families of alcoholics, talked to 9,600 clients in 1984 — an eightfold increase since 1971. In the same period the number of alcoholics helped by the parent organisation 'Alcoholics Anonymous' rose from 6,300 to 34,500.

The number of people turning to marriage guidance organisations for help doubled from 21,600 to 43,700 between 1971 and 1984. The shortage of trained counsellors meant that sometimes people couldn't be seen by a trained counsellor for three months or more. Some marriages ended before help could be offered.

The statistics from the Samaritans also reveal the extent of the need. They were contacted by 87,000 clients in 1971, but this rose to a staggering 358,000 in 1984. The pain which many people feel today is sufficient to drive them to suicide, and if we're not willing to share their pain, we're not fit to follow the Saviour who was willing to die for them.

Through the Helpline I saw that loneliness was prevalent among many different groups of people throughout our area. Elderly people too infirm or too scared to go out would call our Helpline under any pretence 'for a chat'. Some of our callers were young mums at home with small children and they felt distraught and isolated.

Many lonely men also phoned us admitting that they were divorcees who missed the companionship of wife and children. Yvonne Roberts, in her detailed research project into the social needs of men, studied the isolation in which many men live their lives.

> Men seem to spend a lot of time talking to each other, but very little time actually saying anything which touches on the reality of the lives that they are living . . . step outside the formula, and talk about emotions, fear, failure, love, joy — and you become a loner, a bit 'soft' — less of a man.'[1]

Many people in our society today exhibit these symptoms. They have acquaintances and they hold conversations, but they have no one to share their lives with. In the suburbs of our cities there are countless people who have no one to care.

As I drove around my area I sometimes felt quite overwhelmed by the need, and I knew that I couldn't carry this burden on my own. Sometimes I had to hand my sense of concern over to the Lord, for it was just too great to bear.

Jesus loves the world with a depth of compassion we can't begin to understand. This came home to me one evening in Jerusalem when our pilgrimage group paused to look over that beautiful city. It was Holy Week, and we'd been considering the way of the cross. One evening at sunset, we stood on the Mount of Olives and looked down at Jerusalem. We remembered the time when Jesus looked over the city during his last visit, and wept: 'Jerusalem! Jerusalem! You kill the prophets and stone the messengers that God has sent you! How many times have I wanted to put my arms around all your people, just as a hen gathers her chicks under her wings, but you would not let me!' (Mt 23:37).

Jesus had an aching burden for the people of that great city. He knew their needs and wanted to embrace them in his love. These were no empty sentiments, but the expression of One who lived totally for others. He really did care for them all.

As we pause to look over our 'view of the world', we talk together of specific situations of suffering. There may be things which we've read of in the newspaper or seen on television. Or there might be needs which we know personally in our local community. If we're in a group it's important to ensure that this doesn't become an opportunity for gossip, and that no confidences are broken.

During this time of sharing we may begin to feel overwhelmed by the suffering of the world. As we look down on our 'view of the world', however, it's a great strength to remember that although we haven't enough love for the world — Jesus has! We can only really cope by allowing his love to flow through us.

Before we turn to prayer it might be good for us to spend some moments in silence. Very often when we begin to intercede for others our prayers become a kind of shopping list of requests. True intercession shouldn't be like that at all, we should actually 'feel' the needs of those we're praying for.

I believe that we can only pray effectively if we have a genuine concern for those who are the subject of our prayers. Too many of us pray from the mind, but not from the heart. We pause to identify with the needs of those we are to pray for. During this time of silence we ask the Lord for a genuine spirit of compassion and a sense of guidance in how to pray effectively.

True intercession transcends words. As Paul wrote: 'In the same way the Spirit comes to help us, weak as we are. For we do not know how we ought to pray; the Spirit himself pleads with God for us in groans that words cannot express' (Rom 8:26).

Sadly, many of us remain a respectable distance from those who suffer, we pray without aching with love for those in need. The life of Jesus demonstrated that he was willing to be completely immersed in human suffering. His coming among us shows how sharply his values contrast with those of our society.

At his birth Jesus 'emptied himself' and 'humbled himself'. He left the riches of heaven for a stable and a refugee family and became incarnate in human poverty. 'You know the grace of our Lord Jesus Christ; rich as he was, he made himself poor for your sake, in order to make you rich by means of his poverty' (2 Cor 8:9). He was made flesh, and in so doing became frail and vulnerable.

During his life he was nicknamed the 'friend of publicans and sinners', and he shrank from no one. He cared for cheap crooks like Zacchaeus, those of dubious morals like the woman of Samaria, and outcasts like the ten lepers.

Jesus relinquished his power and became powerless. He was willing to taste the unfairness of persecution, the pain of torture and the humiliation of the cross in order to demonstrate his total commitment to those in need. Jesus didn't deal in pious platitudes, or just sympathise with those who suffer — he actually became incarnate in human need.

Os Guinness summed it all up when he wrote:

> Identification is at the heart of the Incarnation. As God became man in Jesus, he was no Whitehall or Pentagon chief, making quick flying inspections to the front line, but one who shared the foxholes, who knew the risks, who felt the enemy fire. No other God has wounds . . . It is when Christians have at least partially entered into the profundity of identification that the Christian community has been at its most human and most sensitive and that its message has been most credible and compelling.'[2]

Because we follow this Servant King we cannot remain distant from the needs of those around us. The life of Jesus was one long demonstration of compassion — love in action. As we prepare ourselves to intercede for the world we move from seeing the suffering around us to feeling it. Only when we 'weep with those who weep' will we be truly ready to intercede for the world.

If we are in a group we may care to stand in a line and hold hands facing our 'view of the world'. With eyes open wide we pray for the different situations we've identified, knowing that the Lord hears and answers. These are not meaningless words; they are 'cries from the heart' to a loving heavenly Father who will move in ways beyond our understanding.

I believe implicitly in the power of prayer. On many occasions I have seen situations turned around by the intercessions of God's people. I believe that prayer should be faith-filled and specific, we should dare to ask God for things and not offer prayers full of 'ifs', 'buts' or 'maybes'. Some prayers of intercession are so full of 'get out' clauses that they require hardly any faith at all!

God may say 'no' to our requests, but we should ask boldly and confidently through the love of Jesus Christ. I don't find this easy myself, but I know it works. Recently I was with a group who were praying that a young man would be able to sell his house. He and his family had moved to a new town, but were unable to buy a new home because they hadn't been able to sell their previous one for over a year.

One of my friends began the prayer meeting by asking the Lord to sell the house within forty-eight hours! Everything in me said 'hold on, that's a bit rash!' I would have prayed for a three-month sale, or maybe even for three-weeks . . . but forty-eight hours! No one was more astounded than me when the man 'phoned to say that he'd sold the house in forty hours!

As we cry out to the Lord in prayer, we believe that Jesus Christ brings our petitions to the heavenly Father. He is at the right hand of God interceding for us, and we have access to the Father through him. Our prayers should end with the words 'in the name of Jesus' because it is through his name that we approach the Father and by whose love we have the confidence that prayer really works.

But prayer must never be a cop-out. As we pray, we may see that we are part of the answer to our prayer. I think we've trivialised the story of the Good Samaritan and that its familiarity has reduced its impact. The priest saw the mugged and beaten traveller and yet 'walked on by'; the Levite actually went over and looked at the man and then 'walked on by'. Both had excuses for pressing on but no real reason for doing so. I have no doubt that they felt sorry for this unfortunate victim, but their sympathy was not translated into practical action. They probably would have prayed for him — but nothing more.

Many of us find it easier to express sympathy than to offer practical help. Now, perhaps more than in any previous generation, our natural instinct is to avoid 'getting involved'. We may feel sorry for people — we may even pray for them, but if we leave them by the wayside we've not 'loved our neighbour as ourselves'.

Colin Morris wrote:

> Because the Gospel is simple, the judgement is immediate. I saw a starving man and there was no gnawing pain in my belly. I saw a hunchback and my own back did not ache. I watched a pathetic procession of refugees being herded back and forth sleeplessly — and I slept well that night. Our failure towards the little people of the earth is more than a lapse of simple charity for which contrition can atone.[3]

Recently I met some young Christians who had carried buckets full of water for five miles one Sunday afternoon. They had carried these heavy buckets so that they could begin to understand what people in drought-stricken areas must do each day.

That evening they staggered into church with their water buckets and offered members of the congregation a glass of the water they'd carried. This 'pilgrimage with a purpose' helped the congregation to understand the needs of those who live in drought-ridden areas and to pray with greater commitment for those who dig wells for them.

Their action was also a trigger for that congregation to offer practical support to those people far away. They had understood the problem for the first time and they began to give generously towards the well-sinking project. Their understanding had led to prayer, and prayer had led to action.

Jesus wanted his followers to have this kind of spontaneous generosity about their lifestyle, an attitude which often contrasts sharply with the way of the world. He said, 'if someone takes you to court to sue you for your shirt, let him have your coat as well. And if one of the occupation troops forces you to carry his pack one kilometre, carry it two kilometres' (Mt 5:40–41).

William Stringfellow wrote that 'a Christian looks like a sucker because he is free to give his life. To die — imminently — for the sake of anyone or anything at all, even for those or that which seems unworthy of his death, thereby celebrating the one who died for all . . . though none be worthy, not even one.'

There's no room for apathy when we follow the Suffering Servant. We are all called to do our part to alleviate the suffering of the world around us. It isn't enough to pray for people if we can do something practical, too. We need to get involved with the needs of people and to respond to them where they are.

There are times when we've all been so eager to 'receive a blessing' that we've failed to 'be a blessing'. Many of us have grown apathetic toward the needs of others. The sheer strain of life and the pressures of family and business have blunted our practical concern for those who suffer.

David Sheppard, the Bishop of Liverpool, and a leading campaigner for the poor, wrote:

> The Incarnation meant truly entering into a world where there was indignation, corrupt authority, sickness, adultery, betraying, agony and bloody sweat. If we can believe that

> God is really incarnate, He is frighteningly close; then He meets us where we are. The followers of Jesus have to live in that world too; like Him we are called to meet people where they are.[4]

All true followers of Jesus are called to meet people where they are. We may have known great experiences of worship, but if our hearts are hard and stoney towards those who need our help, our praise is nothing more than empty noise. Matthew 25 reminds us that Christianity without compassion is blasphemy:

> And he will say to those on his left . . . 'Away from me, you that are under God's curse! . . . I was hungry but you would not feed me, thirsty but you would not give me a drink, I was a stranger but you would not welcome me in your homes, naked but you would not clothe me, I was sick and in pain but you would not take care of me.

Some of us have not yet discovered the wonder of Christian service or the joy of caring for those in need. We've missed countless opportunities for compassion, and we need to ask the Lord for forgiveness and for grace to serve those in need.

It's easy to feel so swamped by the needs of the world that we don't do anything! I have recently returned from Manila in the Philippines, where the homelessness, hunger and poverty of the local people has left me shell-shocked and sad.

In my own life I am trying to work out what I can do practically, while recognising that I can't take on the needs of the world singlehanded.

Every Christian must attempt to face up to the needs that they are aware of and to ask the Lord what they can do in the way of service. In the kingdom of God we are all called to give — but none of us can do everything. Some Christians overcommit themselves and end up exhausted, drained and ineffective . . . and that neither glorifies God nor serves the long-term needs of those around us.

As we move off towards the next section of our pilgrimage, it would be great if we could think about our response to the needs of the world. As we walk along we may care to commit ourselves to some practical act of service for those we have prayed about.

Moving from sympathy to activity is always a difficult step. For as we pray for shut-ins we may find God calling us to visit them; and as we pray for the hungry we might end up giving our money. Having identified the need it isn't easy to become part of the solution — but it's always worth while.

Organising a church pilgrimage

Route five: from the wilderness to the view.
Aim: to pray for the world more effectively.

The view chosen for this part of the pilgrimage should, ideally, be over a small town. As a symbol of communities all over the world, it should help the group to talk about the needs of people who live nearby or far away.

If it isn't possible to look over a town, any hilltop view can give inspiration for intercessory prayer. By looking down on an area of land we can picture God's love for the world more clearly.

On some pilgrimages it may not be possible for the group to see a panoramic view. In this case the group could carry a large flask of water and share a symbolic act of footwashing. As the different members of the

group wash each other's feet there should be discussion about the role of servanthood followed by prayer for those in need. This group could also make some kind of new commitment to serve the needy back home.

It is important that intercessory prayer and practical service are always linked. It can sometimes be an escape from responsibility to pray for those in need, but not to serve them in practical ways too. Christian service unsupported by prayer is powerless, and prayer which does not result in practical service is misguided. Those who pray and who serve have glimpsed God's view of the world.

This section of the pilgrimage should be unhurried. It often takes time for people to share important prayer requests. It also takes time to enter into the suffering of those we're bringing to the Lord.

Those who are leading this section need to demonstrate by what they pray that they believe that prayer changes things. It is important that a 'tone of faith' is set for the group to follow; and that the whole group reinforces each prayer with loud and believing 'AMENS'! Some Christians have never really experienced a faith-filled prayer time, and this is an ideal opportunity for sharing one together.

Organising a personal pilgrimage

Prayers of intercession

All Christians need to make space for intercession. The Holy Spirit guides us in our thinking and articulates those prayers which are too deep for words. We believe that prayer can change things, and that there is no situation beyond the reach of God's love.

Preparation

We should begin by praising God for who he is and what he can do so that our requests are set in the context of faith. It is also good to thank the Lord for previous answers to prayer. Intercessions can easily become lists of requests; but we should avoid doing this. Each request should be brought to the Lord with the 'ache' of understanding as a genuine cry from the heart. This takes time and effort: intercession can be a tiring and demanding activity.

Activity

We stand and look over a town or village, picturing the heartache and suffering behind many of the doors. This town is a symbol of 'hurting' communities all around the world.

Practical advice

(1) Praise God that he is already present in each situation, and thank him that he is already at work in the hearts and lives of those involved.
(2) Before bringing each request to the Lord, picture the situation and detail the different needs you see.
(3) Ask the Lord for specific answers, while recognising that he may choose to work in a different way.
(4) Recognise that your prayer may lead to practical action — and that you may be part of the solution!
(5) Don't try to pray for too many things at once. Four or five prayer requests may be ample to begin with.

Personal follow-up

Keep a prayer diary for a few weeks or months to chart your progress in the ministry of intercession. Keep a short daily list of situations you are concerned about, one for Mondays another for Tuesdays and so on.

Make sure that there is a balance between local needs and needs around the world. Leave ample space beneath each list to write up how the Lord has dealt with each request. Each week turn back and make a note of any specific answers you've seen. From time to time delete requests and add new ones.

If there is a prayer meeting in your church, join it! If not, ask your minister about starting one. Make sure that your housegroup or youth fellowship give time for intercession, and that the congregation is involved in suggesting prayer requests for worship.

Join with two or three friends on a regular basis to pray for specific needs and to praise God for answers received.

Notes

1 Yvonne Roberts, *Man Enough* (Chatto and Windus: London, 1984).
2 Os Guinness, *The Dust Of Death* (Intervarsity Press: Leicester, 1973), pp 387–88.
3 Colin Morris, *Include Me Out* (Fontana/Collins: London, 1975).
4 David Sheppard, *Bias to the Poor* (Hodder and Stoughton: London, 1983).

6
The Pilgrim Community

A pilgrimage tends to throw together many different kinds of people. It's a common experience which breaks down all the social barriers. The strong sense of community that develops on a pilgrimage encourages people to support and encourage one another and to forge relationships that will last for many years.

A pilgrimage group is rather like an extended family, and if there are children present it's sometimes difficult to work out who they belong to! When Mary and Joseph were heading for home after their pilgrimage to Jerusalem they assumed that Jesus was somewhere among the crowd, but after a day they discovered they'd left their twelve-year-old behind. When I took my six-year-old son on a pilgrimage a few weeks ago, it was wonderful to see how the whole group accepted him and how quickly he felt a part of this big happy family.

Bamber Gascoigne, reviewing medieval pilgrimages, wrote: 'A party of pilgrims set out with just as much excitement as a package tour today, and they would have been just as varied a group of people.'[1] Yet these diverse groups of people quickly formed themselves into 'pilgrim bands' and defended one another against the robbers who stalked the pilgrim routes.

A couple of years ago I took a pilgrim group to Israel. I was deeply concerned about the mix of age groups in the tour party. The youngest was four while the oldest was well over eighty-years of age. There were young intellectuals and middle-aged housewives; mature Christians and others just starting out with the Lord. Yet although these people came from such a diverse range of backgrounds, they became one of the strongest fellowships I have ever known.

The oldest member of our party was hardly able to walk at all, so we borrowed a wheelchair and the rest of the group pushed, pulled, carried and lifted her over many miles of pilgrimage. She didn't want to miss anything — and the rest of the group was determined that she didn't.

Some of the friendships within the group crossed all the social barriers. People who would never have chosen each other as friends were thrown together for ten days, and discovered that they actually liked each other! The fellowship times each evening which were scheduled to last forty minutes lasted for hours; we couldn't persuade people to go to bed.

Such was the sense of common identity and unity that we thought nothing of singing 'Jubilate' as we danced round baggage reclaim at Heathrow airport! The pilgrimage had forged links among us which were beautiful and lasting.

Christopher Drummond identified the same kind of experience on a one-day pilgrimage to Dorchester.

Hundreds and hundreds of people take part, of all ages, so it is a great occasion for meeting others; we can walk at a pace that suits us and as we do some will overtake us, while we will overtake others. This gives a wonderful opportunity for meeting new people and for renewing old friendships.

It is interesting to note that the leaders of the churches have called the next phase of the ecumenical process 'Not Strangers But Pilgrims'. One way of encouraging closer links between local churches would be to organise an inter-church pilgrimage as part of a commitment to this wider ecumenical programme.

Pilgrimages are often more ecumenical than they used to be and they can help break down the barriers between different Christians. As a group of Christians from different churches walk together they can learn from the different devotional traditions represented, and build links which formal ecumenical schemes could never achieve.

It's good to invite everyone on a pilgrimage. The group should reflect a wide age range, social background and spiritual maturity. There should be times when everyone walks together . . . and times when smaller groups can share their faith and worship more deeply.

Although a pilgrimage should be great fun and provide plenty of opportunity for informal conversation and sharing, it shouldn't deteriorate into a hilarious romp. There is a serious purpose to the journey, and there needs to be a fine balance between informality and order.

John Bromyard, an English Dominican, wrote critically about the behaviour of some medieval pilgrims:

There are some who keep their pilgrimages not for God but for the devil. They who sin more freely when away from home or who go on pilgrimage to succeed in inordinate and foolish love — those who spend their time on the road in evil and uncharitable conversation may indeed be making their pilgrimage away from God and to the Devil.

True pilgrimages have always had a sense of warmth and friendship, and yet allowed space for times of silence and reverence. Good pilgrimages provide an atmosphere for prayer and devotion, but that doesn't mean they need be boring. There should be a pleasant mix of 'free time' for conversation and 'organised activity' when different aspects of prayer are explored.

Singing can also help to build up a sense of community as the group walks along. Music has always been an important part of pilgrimage and many fragments of pilgrim songs have survived from as long ago as medieval times. But singing can be a distraction as well as a help on a pilgrimage. In 1407 the Lollard William Thorpe complained that the singing of the pilgrims was more of a commotion than a great hymn of praise to the Lord!

They have with them both men and women that can well sing wanton songs, and some other pilgrims will have with them bagpipes; so that every town they come through, what with the noise of their singing, and with the sound of their piping, and with the jangling of their Canterbury bells, and with the barking of dogs after them, that they make more noise, than if the king came their way, with his clarions, and many other minstrels. And if these men and women be a half year out in their pilgrimage, many of them shall be, great janglers, taletellers, and liars.

It's easy for singing to deteriorate into a raucous noise, particularly if everyone's in a good mood. If the pilgrims want to sing as they walk they should try to enhance the atmosphere of prayer rather than create a noisy distraction.

Many songs are suitable for pilgrimage — such as the triumphant choruses of Graham Kendrick, or the traditional hymns of Wesley and Watts. The music used by the brothers of Taizé is particularly inspirational. Each song is very simple — a few words chanted to a lovely plainsong. As the words gradually sink into our minds, our hearts are opened to pray. These songs are used by thousands of young pilgrims who gather every summer at the Taizé community in France.

One pilgrim to Taizé, a girl from Berlin, summed up her impressions: 'It was just at the time of my life when I had more or less rejected everything to do with the church. But the church services in Taizé simply bowled me over. The intensity of the prayer, the singing, the silence — it was all new to me. Taizé wakened so much in me that I decided to come again.'

Worship songs on the themes of the pilgrimage could be selected and introduced to the walkers before the event. Guitars and other portable instruments should be taken wherever possible, and the pilgrims invited to sing as they walk. Christian fellowship is deeper than the friendships which form between members of a rambling association or hiking club. On this walk we are celebrating the fact that we share a common experience of Christ and a sense of belonging to the family of God.

One of the hallmarks of a pilgrimage is this sense of belonging to one another. It's a quality which can't be taught or regulated; it comes as a gift of the Holy Spirit. As the pilgrims walk along together they are aware that Jesus walks with them, and that he is the silent listener to every conversation.

A pilgrimage offers a wonderful opportunity for people to exercise a ministry of encouragement to one another. It's good to thank God for the others in the group, and to build one another up in all that we say and do. The pilgrim group should be a living example of what the church should always be — a caring and sensitive community.

Many of us have yet to discover what 'belonging to the family of God' really means. We need to understand that we haven't chosen one another but God has adopted us and united us with Christ. This was powerfully illustrated for me some years ago when some people came to visit us.

The doorbell rang at home, and I went to greet some of my closest friends. This married couple had come to stay with us, but it was no ordinary visit. They had come to London to collect a baby from a nearby adoption agency, and they were very excited.

They had wanted children for some time, and at last they had decided to adopt. The many months of interview and assessment had gone by and at last they were offered a new-born baby. They arrived at our home late one night full of anticipation, and just a little apprehensive!

The following morning they left our house for the wonderful world of 'Mothercare'. They returned several hours later with a car crammed full of things they needed for their new baby.

After lunch they set off for the adoption agency, and late that night they returned with a new-born baby boy. He was a tiny fellow of mixed English and West Indian parentage, and he gurgled happily in his new white shawl.

Seeing them with their new son was a very precious experience. The joy of that couple was quite indescribable. They were welcoming this little stranger to become part of their family. He couldn't buy or earn their love, only receive what they gave. I felt it was a special privilege to share that time with them.

That incident was the most perfect illustration of the

love of God which I've ever seen. Galatians 4:4 reads: 'But when the right time finally came, God sent His own Son. He came as the son of a human mother and lived under the Law, so that we might become God's sons. To show that you are his sons, God sent the Spirit of His Son into our hearts, the Spirit who cries out, "Father, my Father." So then, you are no longer a slave but a son. And since you are His son, God will give you all that He has for His sons.'

It is now about twelve years since that couple came to collect their son from the adoption agency. Recently we met up and went on a family hike around a reservoir together. It was a very muddy walk, and as we squelched along in our wellington boots in the cold wintry drizzle I remembered the day that my friend had adopted his son. And now my son walked beside me, and his son walked beside him, and there was no difference between us. We were both fathers, both sons, both families.

We are all 'adopted' into the family of God through the love of Jesus, and because this is the basis of our faith we have no option but to accept one another. Each group of Christians is a family in Christ among whom there can be no divisions.

As we walk on this pilgrimage we should treat the other walkers like our brothers and sisters in Christ. Our conversation, our caring and our relationships should be a celebration of our oneness together. All Christians are adopted by the same Saviour, and our walk should be a symbol of our unity in him.

Most of us have known rejection at some time or other. The teenager who feels broken-hearted at the end of a romance; the manager who's been made redundant; the girl who wasn't invited to her friend's wedding. But one of the cruellest forms of rejection is racism.

I really appreciated the fellowship of a Sri Lankan family who were members of our church. Their devotion to Christ and their witness within the community was very special.

After church one Sunday morning they took their children to the swings in the park beside the church. They put the two children on the swings and pushed them high into the air. The two small girls laughed with joy! It was one of those happy family times when they were all 'off guard'. They hadn't noticed the gang of youths creeping up on them. They were shocked and startled when the gang taunted, 'Wogs, go home.' and began to throw stones at them.

The parents snatched their children from the swings and ran for safety. A shower of stones flew past them as they ran. This incident frightened the children and shocked their parents. Suddenly they didn't feel safe any more and the children certainly didn't want to visit that park again.

Different people from our church went to visit the family to assure them that we really loved them. One of the hallmarks of a Christian fellowship is that people of all kinds and backgrounds are welcome and accepted. A church which does not welcome everyone equally cannot preach that Christ died for all.

Groups like to turn their backs on individuals, and if there's anything to mark you out and make you different you're an easy target. You may have the wrong colour skin, the wrong kind of accent, the wrong kind of clothes or a handicapped body. You may just be a newcomer. If you can be singled out, you can be rejected.

As we walk on this pilgrimage there might be opportunities for sharing some of the experiences of rejection which we've known, and of celebrating the fact that on this pilgrimage we all belong to one another.

None of us are shielded from experiences of rejection no matter how stable our home life, how secure our career, or however popular we may be within our peer group. It is always painful to be rejected, snubbed, passed over, brushed aside or left on the shelf. For some of us this sense of rejection is so overwhelming that it can deeply affect our lives.

I saw the pain of rejection in the eyes of a young woman I was interviewing for a job. The three of us on the interview panel had been talking to candidates all day. I was feeling really drained and it was hard to concentrate after so long.

I went through the usual small talk and asked her the questions that we'd been asking different interviewees during the day. She was bright and intelligent, and she answered clearly and decisively. I was quite impressed by her answers, but then, without any warning, she burst into tears.

This was a real conversation-stopper and silence fell. The three of us on the panel shuffled our papers in embarrassment. We tried to make the right sympathetic noises but there was an awkwardness about the situation which was difficult to overcome.

Eventually she wiped her eyes with a tissue and said: 'I'm a graduate and a trained teacher. I've been out of college for over eighteen months but I've never had an interview, let alone a job. I've lost all my confidence and I don't know where to turn.'

This was just one person in a long line of unemployed people we'd talked to that day. I couldn't get their faces out of my mind for days afterwards. The world deals harshly with people, and rejection is rife.

Yet the Christian sees people differently. Each person

has special God-given gifts, each one is of supreme value in his kingdom, and each one has a role which only they can fulfil. We see each other as unique individuals each with a special contribution to make, and not by the standards of the job market.

Sadly, some churches seem to offer a ministry of discouragement — and I've actually seen Christians put one another down. In our conversation on this pilgrimage there should be no 'competitive spirit' among us and no desire to 'outdo' one another. As we walk along we should seek to encourage the others in the group and to value them as precious children of God.

Christian fellowship should be supportive and caring, a kind of safety net which surrounds each member of the church. There will be times when we all need the support of fellow-believers.

The 'phone rang late one night and a voice I didn't recognise told me that a dear friend of mine was very sick. He had been rushed home from the mission-field gravely ill, and was being cared for in the London Hospital for Tropical Diseases. I went to see him late the following day.

It was night time and the nurses were chatting in the ward reception area. I explained that I was a minister and that I wished to see my friend. I was told that he was too ill to see me, so I opted for standing beside his cubicle window and giving him a wave!

When he saw me at the window he rang his bedside bell and explained to the nurse that he wanted to see me. I quickly donned a cap, mask and gown and strode into the little glass cubicle. He was very ill and his temperature was high. There seemed little to say, but he whispered, 'Please Rob, pray for me.'

I prayed for him there and then, and enlisted Christian

friends around the country to offer prayer support day and night. Weeks later, when he began to regain his strength, he thanked me for this prayer support. 'When you feel as ill as I did,' he explained, 'you can't pray for yourself, you just glide along on the prayers of others.'

This is the kind of support that Christian fellowship should offer. We are sometimes too weak, too broken or too low to pray. At times like that we can only ride on the love and prayers of the fellowship to which we belong. Unfortunately some churches don't seem to take this ministry seriously, and some Christians haven't grasped its importance.

There have been times in my own ministry when I have felt exhausted or dried up, and I have been greatly blessed by the knowledge that others were praying for me. I've also known many pastoral situations where people in major crises have been 'carried' through dark days by the prayers of those around them.

In the parable of the friend at midnight, Jesus made it clear that we should be persistent in prayer. The man who appeared at the door at midnight kept on asking for a loaf of bread, and in the end he was successful. Part of our calling as Christians is to be faithful in prayer, and to keep on asking until an answer comes.

If we are with a group it might be good to talk together about the ministry of prayer. Some of the group may be able to share testimonies of times when they've been 'carried' by the prayers of others. To reinforce this point it may be good to carry someone in the group. Great care must be taken in doing this, and the person carried should relax completely and allow his/her fellow-pilgrims to 'take the weight'. Afterwards, he/she should describe how it felt, and the group should then talk together about the prayer support they would like to see in their local church.

When we were clearing out an old cupboard in the first church I pastored in Yorkshire, we came across a loving-cup. It was a large mug, about a century old. I did some research and discovered that since the times of Wesley the people called Methodists had held regular 'love-feasts'. They were times when the church gathered to share testimonies and to exhort one another to a deeper walk with Christ. You could only attend a lovefeast when you produced your 'membership ticket' and these meetings were considered some of the most precious times of fellowship by the early Methodists.

We began to hold lovefeasts in our chapels, much along the lines of those which had been organised in our area a century before, and we used the same old loving-cup. They turned out to be powerful times of sharing, and everyone felt encouraged and strengthened in the faith.

It was our privilege to lead the first ever televised lovefeast, and people wrote in from all over the country to say how much they had been blessed by the love and fellowship in the group.

If we are walking with a group, we pause to share a simple lovefeast as a symbol of our love and fellowship. One of the hallmarks of pilgrimage has been the gathering together of small groups along the wayside for fellowship, sharing and worship. At this point on the pilgrimage, then, we pause for a time of fellowship in some suitable setting. It may be a clearing, a clifftop or a beach, but this beautiful place will become as sacred to us as a grand cathedral.

The worship begins with some suitable praise songs. When the group is relaxed and feels at one, each member asks another to pray something specific for them. True fellowship means lifting one another up and everyone present should be prayed for.

Following this time of prayer the 'pilgrim loaf' is passed around. It is important that everyone present realises that this is not Holy Communion but a lovefeast. As the bread is passed around, each person tears off a piece and eats it. No words are spoken.

This sharing of the loaf is a symbol of our belonging to one another because we all belong to the one who is the Bread of life. This time should be a time of silent encouragement, support and love. We can sometimes say more with our eyes than our mouths.

Next the common cup is passed around. All the pilgrims drinking from the same cup is a symbol of their unity in the Lord. This is also done in silence and it may be good to pray silently for each person as they take the cup.

The richness of fellowship which we share in this beautiful setting should be carried back to our home churches. A congregation should pray for each other and support each other practically and spiritually through hard times. When it does so, a love grows up among them which the world cannot understand or imitate.

At the end of this time of fellowship, the group says together the prayer which belongs to the family of the church. Very often we say this quickly or thoughtlessly, but on this occasion it is said slowly and with much meaning:

Our Father, who art in heaven,
hallowed be thy Name;
thy kingdom come;
thy will be done;
on earth as it is in heaven.

Give us this day our daily bread.
And forgive us our trespasses,
as we forgive those who trespass against us.
And lead us not into temptation;
but deliver us from evil.
For thine is the kingdom,
the power, and the glory,
for ever and ever. Amen.

As the group leaves this place of fellowship it might be good for them to promise one another that they will support each other in prayer. The bonds of fellowship developed on this pilgrimage could be a rich blessing over the months and years that lie ahead.

Organising a church pilgrimage

Route six: from the view to the clearing.

Aim: to demonstrate the importance of praying for one another.

Members of the group may have known times of hurtful rejection in their past. As we walk along, it may be possible to share something of this pain, and to demonstrate our support and love for one another.

It can be great fun to carry someone, but also rather hard work! However, it's worth doing this activity as it powerfully communicates the importance of carrying one another in prayer. Great care should be taken in this exercise, and it may be wisest to carry the lightest person in the group!

A four-handed seat can be made when two strong people each grasp their left wrist with their right hand. They grasp the right wrist of the other pilgrim with their left hand. The person being carried supports himself by sitting on the 'seat' constructed and by holding onto the shoulders of the two carriers.

It would geatly enhance the time of fellowship if the site chosen were particularly beautiful. Plastic sheeting could be carried for people to sit on, and it would be great if there were some benches available for older folk.

The bread to be shared at the lovefeast can be any small loaf; but currant loaves or spiced buns would more closely resemble the pilgrim loaves of medieval times. If it is possible to use a proper loving-cup, so much the better, but if not a simple bowl would be quite adequate.

After the bread and water have been shared it may be helpful if the pilgrims move into smaller groups for a time of sharing and prayer for one another. People will often share deeply in fours or fives, but in a larger group they are unlikely to do so. This section of the pilgrimage can take up a lot of time, and the leader should ensure that this period of sharing and prayer doesn't delay the itinerary too much.

There may be members of the group who are in the midst of some deep personal crisis at this time. If this is the case it is important that they are in a prayer group supervised by a mature leader, and that a great deal of support is given to them.

Throughout the pilgrimage it may well be hard to keep the balance between times of fun and times of serious devotion. If the group members become too light-headed the devotional element will be lost, but if they become too intense and serious it is likely that some of them will become bored.

The balance is best kept by limiting the times of devotion and teaching to the different 'markers' or 'locations' on the route. The walk between each of these should probably be less structured and more informal. It is important to remember that Jesus is just as much with us in hilarity and chatter as he is in times of meditation and devotion.

Organising a personal pilgrimage

Prayer

It's not only world leaders or overseas missionaries who need prayer support — we all need it! When we know that others are praying for us and that we are surrounded by a safety net of care and love, we can find the strength to face many difficulties. Part of the joy of belonging to a Christian fellowship is to pray for others and to know that they are praying for us. In this section of our personal pilgrimage we need to spend time sharing with one or two other Christians.

Preparation

It is difficult to develop this kind of prayer support relationship with lots of people. Better to choose one or two at the most. It may be our marriage partner or someone in the church with whom we have a real affinity. Before we can discover the joy of prayer support, we need to get to know one another and to share those areas of our lives where we are most vulnerable. Those who support one another need to learn how to laugh together and cry together and how to share their innermost needs with one another.

Activity

When two people physically carry a third we discover something of the relationship which develops in prayer support. It is good actually to do this and then discuss how it felt.

Practical advice

(1) It's good for people in a prayer support relationship to be married to one another or of the same sex.
(2) Try to make a regular time and place for meeting, perhaps once a month or more.
(3) Spend time talking about what's been happening in your life, and don't hide things which you're ashamed of.
(4) Pray for one another daily; phone each other if you have some special need or crisis.
(5) Rejoice together at what God has been doing in your lives, and thank him for situations resolved, crises overcome and needs supplied!

Personal follow-up:

Regularly take stock of your relationship with your 'prayer supporter' and move on to a new prayer partner if you feel the time is right.

Notes

1 Bamber Gascoigne, *The Christians* (Cape: London, 1986).

7
The Road to the Cross

When I was a teenager I used to go on an annual pilgrimage through Birmingham city centre. Every Good Friday I joined hundreds of young people on this march. At the front of the procession was a large cross carried by young people from the different churches.

No words were spoken or songs sung as we walked past the Easter shoppers and the noisy city traffic. It was a powerful experience and I was drawn closer to God through it. We were celebrating the death of one who died for us, and our silent pilgrimage said it all.

We moved from church to church around the city and paused at each to read some section of the Good Friday story and to sing a hymn. The cross we carried was a poignant reminder of Christ's saving love and his invitation to 'take up the cross, deny self and follow me'.

Processions such as this are reminiscent of the earliest Christian pilgrimages. The pilgrims walked from site to site around the Holy Land, reading from Scripture and saying prayers. Gradually some simple liturgies developed, and groups used a different service at each place. Professor

Hunt described these liturgies as 'a form of worship distinguished by its movement and arduous length'. The Eastern church began to use these Holy Land liturgies as the basis for pilgrimage in many towns and villages.

This ancient tradition continues in many different forms, and every Easter countless churches around the world carry a cross and follow a simple liturgy as they process around their town. In Lancashire a group from all the local churches climb to the top of a large hill above their town to erect a cross. The cross stands there throughout the Easter period as a constant reminder of the death and resurrection of Jesus Christ. Its huge structure dominates the skyline, a silent witness to an age-old story.

The cross is a powerful symbol, and its stark simple shape communicates more about the love of God than words can ever convey. Many pilgrims have 'carried the cross' as a symbol of their devotion to the Lord and their gratitude for his sacrifice on Calvary. The cross symbolises the rejection of the world. 'The Word was in the world, and though God made the world through him, yet the world did not recognize him. He came to his own country, but his own people did not receive him' (Jn 1:10).

The cross reminds us that the soldiers beat Jesus, mocked him, and placed a crown of thorns on his head: they had perfected suffering to a fine art. They led him up the hill of Calvary and nailed him to a cross. He died despised and rejected by all. But the cross also reminds us of the love of God. The cross declares God's love and forgiveness for all: 'For God loved the world so much that he gave his only Son, so that everyone who believes in him may not die but have eternal life.'

One of the most well-known pilgrimages 'with a cross'

in recent years has been undertaken by the American evangelist Arthur Blessitt. He has made symbolic pilgrimages around the world for many years, and wherever he goes he carries a ten-foot cross mounted on small wheels. He has dragged it across deserts, through city streets and over whole continents. Wherever Arthur goes, the cross goes too!

When trundling his cross through some of the thickest jungle in the world Arthur was guided by a group of tribal folk who knew the way. As he went, he came across some *National Geographic* explorers going where 'no white man had ever been before'. They were shocked and astounded to see him carrying his cross through 'impenetrable jungle', and followed him and his cross.

He has sat with his cross in the centre of trouble spots in Belfast, and on the peace line in Lebanon. He's carried it into the state rooms of many of the world's most powerful leaders. It has become a talking point on chat shows and television newscasts all over the world.

Wherever he goes his simple message remains the same, it's a message of forgiveness for sin, reconciliation between enemies and hope for the world. Arthur Blessitt believes that the cross is the solution to all our personal needs and to the needs of the whole world. He carries a cross because it declares the love of God to every people and culture.

Towards the close of our pilgrimage we make a large cross out of rough branches found by the wayside. As we make this cross, we should remember what the cross means to us, and the pain and rejection which it symbolises.

We may discover something more of what the cross says about suffering. Some pilgrims go on a journey to ask questions about suffering. I have known people to go on long walks when they've been through some experience of personal tragedy or bereavement in order to seek the mind of God and understand more of his ways.

When I was a theological student helping to run a daily 'phone-in on BBC Radio Manchester I was contacted by a young curate who wanted to make a pilgrimage across the Sahara Desert. At first I thought he was quite mad, or at least a bit eccentric, but the more I talked to him the more convinced I became that this was a serious mission.

Part of his reason for wanting to do the walk was to raise money for charity, but he was also motivated by a strong desire to draw closer to God and to struggle with some of his deepest questions about life. He felt that by walking across that vast empty expanse he would be able to focus on the Lord and wrestle with his questions in prayer. He felt that he needed a support crew to be nearby in case anything went wrong, but he couldn't find any volunteers. Through our radio programme we were able to arrange for a team of British soldiers to follow him in a Land-Rover and help him if he ran into any difficulty.

Several months later he set off from Manchester after a national press conference and began his pilgrimage across the desert. It took him many weeks to complete, but he didn't have any problems and didn't have to call on his 'rescue team'.

I spent an evening with him when he got back, and he told me of the intense silences he had known in the middle of the desert. The dramatic feeling of isolation out there had drawn him closer to the Lord, and taught him to rely on God in a much deeper way. He had agonised over the question of suffering as he had endured the intense heat of the desert, and he came back with a fresh understanding that this question is best answered by looking at the Lord suffering for us on the cross.

We may not have the opportunity or the inclination to walk across the Sahara, but we may still wish to use our pilgrimage to meditate on the suffering of the world, and to seek to understand more of the Lord by looking at the cross. As we look up at the cross we remember that deep within the heart of Jesus lies an insight into our every need. He knows just how we feel even when no one else understands.

I went through a time of questioning about suffering in my own life when I was a young minister in Yorkshire. It started when I drove a young Yorkshire family to a big hospital near Leeds. In the back of the car, huddled in a blanket, was a little boy aged three. This child had been a bundle of energy just a few months before, but now he was weak and sickly – and crippled with cancer.

I saw his pale sullen face in my driving mirror. His parents sat in silence as we drove the weary miles to the special children's cancer unit. They knew that his treatment of chemotherapy and radiography would put an enormous strain on him and on his brothers and sisters who loved him so. They didn't know where to turn in their distress.

As we waited in the corridor for the child to be examined, we sat in stony silence. The father walked up the corridor and back, sat down for a while, then walked off again. We watched folk come and go. Time stood still. I could not quote a text, nor make a theological statement. Every argument I'd learnt about 'the problem of pain' or the 'theology of suffering' was silenced. I had nothing to say.

For days afterwards my mind was in turmoil. I asked the Lord to show me why this child had to suffer but there was no blazing answer in the sky nor booming words of wisdom. Just a hollow emptiness. The question of suffering hung heavy on my mind, but again and again one strong image filled my thoughts. I saw the figure of Christ on the cross and heard those piercing words of dereliction, 'My God, my God, why did you abandon me?' I sensed in a new way that even in the extremity of human suffering he was with us; and that even in those bleak moments of despair he was by my side. The cross said it all.

In the anguish of Calvary Jesus not only knew physical pain and torture, he knew complete separation from his heavenly Father. There was no depth of human suffering which Jesus did not experience. He understands.

My visit to the hospital in the centre of Croydon was an unusual one. I was going to visit an older minister who was suffering from a rare blood disease; the prognosis wasn't good.

As I entered the dull Victorian ward he shouted a friendly greeting and shuffled towards me in a bright silk dressing gown. He was very glad to see me, and I him.

You can't do a 'professional' hospital visit with a fellow minister. They know the catchphrases and see through the pleasantries! You talk frankly and deeply. He told me that his time of illness had been a time of learning, and he had much which we wanted to share.

'In all my years as a hospital chaplain' he confided 'I never realised what it was like to be stuck in here. You breeze in and out and say nice things to people, but you're always on the outside looking in. But now, you see, I'm on the inside too.

'I get woken up at some ungodly hour, I suffer those

wretched transfusions every day. I don't know what the future holds – I'm going through the mill as well as all the other patients.

'Because of that the other patients let me get close to them, and let me pray with them. I've done more here in a few weeks than in years of being a hospital chaplain.'

From this experience my friend could understand the Saviour's suffering more clearly, for he concluded 'We have a Saviour living on the inside – he's not a visitor looking in.' The words of Hebrews spoke to me in a powerful new way:

> Our High Priest is not one who cannot feel sympathy with our weaknesses. On the contrary, we have a high priest who was tempted in every way that we are, but did not sin. Let us be brave then, and come forward to God's throne, where there is grace. There we will receive mercy and find grace to help us just when we need it (Heb 4:15).

Alone, or with our pilgrim group, we may wish to pause to bring our deepest hurts, doubts and sorrows to the foot of the cross we have erected — and to remember that as he was crucified Jesus cried 'My God, my God . . . why?' It's good to know that even when answers to our deepest questions evade us, even there is one who understands. But the cross is not only a symbol of suffering, it's the supreme symbol of salvation.

Some of the earliest pilgrims went to live in Jerusalem because they felt that they had failed back home. Jerusalem was seen as a good place to make a new start. This idea gradually developed and by the sixth-century pilgrimage was an accepted way of making atonement for some sin. The length of the pilgrimage depended on the gravity of the sin. By the thirteenth-century convicted criminals were punished by being sent on a pilgrimage! Some of the writers of the time expressed concern that so many violent murderers were walking along the roads to Jerusalem bound in chains.

It is very sad that pilgrimage was seen as a way of earning forgiveness or of paying God for wrongs done. Christian theology teaches that we can never make atonement for our sin, no matter how long our pilgrimage might be. This was done once and for all by Jesus on the cross.

Paul wrote 'By his death we are now put right with God; how much more, then, will we be saved by him from God's anger! We were God's enemies, but he made us his friends through the death of his Son' (Rom 5:9–10).

His death there opened the way for us to return to God. We are forgiven through Christ's redeeming work on the cross, and not through any effort of our own. When Jesus cried 'It is finished' he said it all. He wasn't saying 'I'm finished', but, 'I've finished the work I came to do.' And so the sacrifice was complete. By dying on the cross, Jesus won salvation for us. We receive this salvation as a free gift, for there is nothing we can offer to 'deserve it'.

As we stand before the cross we pause to give silent thanksgiving for the gift of salvation which we have received, and we recognise that nothing we have done can ever buy it.

We then take up the cross and carry it, and are reminded of the life of service and commitment which Jesus asks us to live. When Jesus made his famous invitation to 'take up the cross and deny self' it must have sounded very strange. He was inviting his followers to pick up the symbol of death and walk with it every day. Yet that is the cost of discipleship; and as we feel the weight of the cross, it might be good for us to consider what this cost might involve in our lives.

Our society conditions us to think about ourselves and our own needs first, but Christ would have us 'die to self' and make his kingdom and the good of others our first priority.

When Paul wrote to the people of Rome he was at pains to point out that the Christian life is not about sacrificing animals but about sacrificing one's life in Christ's service.

> So then, my brothers, because of God's great mercy to us I appeal to you: Offer yourselves as a living sacrifice to God, dedicated to his service and pleasing to him. This is the true worship that you offer (Rom 12:1).

As each person 'carries the cross', they might care to rededicate their lives to Christ, and offer a life more given over to God and less taken up with self.

But the cross is also a symbol of the victory that Jesus won over the power of evil. He rose triumphant over the power of suffering, evil and death, and his victory can be ours if only we will claim it.

We plant our cross firmly in the ground and walk on past it. This reminds us that we are living after the resurrection, and that in the risen power of Jesus we have the resources to overcome whatever may defeat us. As we walk beyond the cross we remember that this victory is no airy-fairy dream; it has been worked out in the lives of countless Christians down the centuries.

A few years ago a member of my church was interviewed on a secular radio programme about suffering.

She had just been told that she had terminal cancer and only had a few months left to live. The rather sarcastic young newsman asked her to describe 'how it felt' and 'how she'd cope'.

She confidently explained that in the power and love of Jesus Christ she could face anything. I watched Jessie over the ensuing months, and I saw her pain, her inability to eat and then to drink, her discomfort and her suffering.

On the night she died the ward sister paid tribute to her. In all her suffering she had never complained, never despaired and never been impatient. Her grace and love had affected the whole ward. She had, indeed, claimed the victory of Christ and lived it for all to see.

As we carry the cross we are carrying a symbol of Christ's victory over suffering. In his resurrection he overcame the power of suffering, and opened the way for all Christians to do the same.

I love the story of Corrie Ten Boom's witness in Holland during World War 2. Who could fail to be challenged and encouraged by her testimony of God's strength as a prisoner in Ravensbruck concentration camp? There, in the pit of evil and darkness, she started a prayer and Bible study group. She wrote:

> Like waifs clustered round a blazing fire, we gathered about the Word of God — holding out our hearts to its warmth and light. The blacker the night around us grew, the brighter and more beautiful burned the Word of God as we read, 'In all these things we have complete victory through him who loved us.'[1]

As we carry the cross, we are carrying a symbol of victory over evil. No matter what darkness of evil we face, we can draw on Jesus' risen power to lead us through to victory. We must learn to live in his power day by day, and to understand that his strength is available to us to overcome every kind of temptation which comes our way.

At my mother's funeral in a small Cotswold village chapel the mourners followed the coffin into the country graveyard a small distance away. I never doubted my mother's faith in Jesus, or her conviction that she was saved by the power of the cross. As the large procession wound its way down the village street we sang, 'We're marching to Zion, beautiful, beautiful Zion, We're marching onward to Zion, the beautiful City of God.'

We know his risen power in our dying as well as in our living. As we face death we face it in the victory of his resurrection.The cross is a symbol of our salvation and a promise of eternal life to come.

As we carry the cross, we could pray for the different problems and needs we face, and claim the victory which is ours through the power of Jesus. It is a victory over death, over suffering and over evil; and it is a victory already won.

As Paul wrote:

> I am certain that nothing can separate us from his love; neither death nor life; neither angels nor other heavenly rulers or powers, neither the present nor the future, neither the world above nor the world below — there is nothing in all creation that will ever be able to separate us from the love of God which is ours through Christ Jesus our Lord (Rom 4:15).

Organising a church pilgrimage

Route seven: from the lovefeast to the place of the cross.
Aim: to meditate on the meaning of the cross and to claim the 'victory'.

The group looks around for suitable pieces of timber for a cross. Several pieces could be collected, and the most suitable ones chosen. Many of our churches have ornamental gold or silver crosses; we need to find branches which are stark and gnarled as a contrast.

As the group looks for wood, each person could picture the stark brutality of crucifixion. The cross was used by the Romans to crucify murderers, thieves and terrorists. It was an instrument of death and it epitomised rejection by society.

As the two pieces of wood are lashed together, the discussion focuses on the cross and the rejection that it symbolised. Some strong twine or wire must be used to tie the pieces together, but if a hammer and nails could be carried this would make an even greater impact. It would be good if the group could stand the cross up and try to picture what a crucifixion was like, and to understand something of the pain and suffering it entailed.

The group spends some silent moments looking up at the cross, while the leader reads out some of the words which Jesus spoke from it: 'Father forgive them for they know not what they do'; 'It is finished', or 'My God my God why have you forsaken me?' The group then pauses to reflect on these words in silence.

As the pilgrims walk along with the cross, they think about the commitment involved in following Jesus and the cost of 'taking up the cross' daily. The cross is passed from one member of the group to another as they walk along.

The cross is then firmly planted in the soil and left by the wayside. The group then walk 'beyond the cross' and as they go they claim the victory which is theirs through the risen power of the Lord. Too few of us today know how to pray 'victoriously' and to claim Christ's victory over the different fears and temptations that assail us.

Organising a personal pilgrimage

The prayer of victory

Many of us are living 'defeated' Christian lives. We live as though we have no power to fight temptation, no strength to carry us through suffering, and no hope to overcome death. Our prayers often reflect this 'defeated' attitude. When we pray the prayer of victory, we claim the resources of God for our need, and stand on the promises which Jesus has made for us.

Preparation

Identify areas of your life where you feel you are 'under attack' or 'defeated', and where you would like to see the 'victory of Jesus' at work. (eg, some fear or insecurity, some sin or habit, some wrong attitude or meanness of spirit).

Read, learn and absorb these famous quotations from Romans 8. They are an excellent preparation for praying in victory, and could be whispered or spoken out loud.

> If God is for us, who can be against us?
>
> Who, then, can separate us from the love of Christ?
>
> In all these things we have complete victory through him who loved us!
>
> Nothing in all creation will ever be able to separate us from the love of God which is ours through Jesus Christ our Lord.

Activity

We make a simple wooden cross, and as we make it and stand it up, we claim the victory that Jesus won for us on the cross.

Practical advice

Paul makes a list of areas where we should claim the victory of Christ. Look at each of these areas and identify where you are most under attack at present.

> For I am convinced that neither death nor life, neither angels nor demons, neither the present nor the future, nor any powers, neither height nor depth, nor anything else in all creation, will be able to separate us from the love of God that is in Christ Jesus our Lord (Rom 8:38).

Gather with one or two other Christian friends to claim the victory and to receive the power and grace you need. It's one thing to claim the victory of Christ, it's another to live in it. Some people go on claiming, but they don't receive what God has for them. As you claim the victory, take time to receive God's renewing power and to thank him for it.

Personal follow-up

We must recognise that the Christian life is not a static one. We should be receiving more and more from Jesus, for though we have much, there is always more.

By studying the following verses, we'll see how important it is to grow closer to Christ and to receive the renewing power of the Holy Spirit each day. As we claim the victory of Christ and live in it day by day, we will become more and more like Jesus.

Read Philippians 3:12; 2 Corinthians 3:18; 2 Corinthians 6:13; Ephesians 5:18.

Notes

1 Corrie Ten Boom, *The Hiding Place* (Hodder and Stoughton: London, 1976).

8
Destinations

I once went on a lovely 'mystery trip' organised by a church in Devon. It was a beautiful day, and we enjoyed the journey which took us across the Tamar Bridge and into Cornwall. The route through several fishing villages was delightful, but the destination was a disappointment, for journey's end was the car park of a fish-and-chip shop!

Every pilgrimage should have a destination. When the Jews went on pilgrimage their destination was the Temple in Jerusalem. The Temple represented all that God had done for them in the past, and reminded them of his faithfulness down many generations.

But their destination was also a symbol of hope for the future. For they believed that one day all the nations of the world would gather in the Holy City and that the Lord would reign for ever. Their destination was a foretaste of the Eternal City prepared for all mankind.

The first Christian pilgrims chose Palestine as their destination. They felt that if they walked where Jesus walked they could draw closer to Him. That's why they were willing to make long and dangerous journeys to visit Jerusalem and Galilee.

Gradually, however, other areas grew in popularity and Christian pilgrims looked to the burial places of the Apostles as important destinations for pilgrimage. Sadly, many of these shrines became steeped in myth, superstition and commercialism.

Many pilgrims went to Rome where they could visit the tombs of St Peter or St Paul. Staggering numbers of pilgrims walked, rode or sailed to Rome at a time when travel was slow and difficult. In 1300 there were about 200,000 pilgrims in and around Rome, many of whom had travelled hundreds of miles to get there.

Another popular destination was Santiago de Compostela in Spain. Many believed that the body of St James was buried there, in a nine-towered stone basilica. In 1434 alone, about 2,400 British pilgrims left Bristol, the port of departure for Santiago, to begin the long sea voyage to Spain.

Gradually more and more English destinations for pilgrimage emerged. Thousands made a solemn pilgrimage to Norwich Cathedral as a mark of respect for a boy called William. Many Norfolk people thought that he'd been ritually murdered in 1144 and regarded him as a saint, even though he was not canonised. His reputation rapidly spread and soon people from the length and breadth of the country wanted to visit his tomb.

In the South of England, Canterbury emerged as a popular place of pilgrimage. A shrine was opened there twelve months after the murder of Archbishop Thomas Beckett in the cathedral. Many believed that they could find physical healing in this place, and monks recorded between 200 and 400 miracles in the cathedral between 1170 and 1180.

Durham emerged as a popular pilgrimage centre in the North of England. At this cathedral the pilgrims could visit the tomb of Godric of Finchale, a venerated hermit who had lived about three miles from the city. Many healing miracles were also recorded at Durham.

Pilgrimages to shrines of the Virgin Mary were common in the Eastern church from the days of the early church, but there was no mention of them in the Western church until the tenth century. From this time, various relics of her hair or clothing were said to be housed in shrines at places like Walsingham, Ipswich, Lincoln and Leicester.

It is difficult for us today to understand the attraction of these destinations to such vast numbers of people. But these were days of very primitive medicine and many people went on these pilgrimages to find a cure for their physical or mental problems.

Relics of the saints, especially their skulls, were considered to be of great importance in this healing process. Pilgrims believed that some mystic force was emitted by these objects, and that anyone standing nearby would grow 'heavier' because they were soaked in this 'aura', and that this process would enable healing to take place. Many people claimed that they were miraculously healed at these shrines, and monks often kept careful records of the healings which pilgrims described.

Often the opening of a shrine brought great prosperity to the local church. New building projects could be undertaken because of the donations of the pilgrims. The bodies of 'saints' were sometimes divided up between several shrines so that more pilgrims could benefit and more money be raised.

Collections at Cantilupe's shrine in Hereford meant that the nave of the cathedral could be enlarged. The front of the beautiful church at St Albans was built with proceeds from the shrine of St Amphibalus, and the monks of Gloucester rejoiced at the income from the shrine of Edam II.

A whole 'pilgrimage industry' grew up around the shrines, and it was possible to buy 'relics' and souvenirs of a pilgrimage. Inns prospered along the different pilgrim routes, and robbers stalked the pilgrims wherever they went.

Some people went on pilgrimage to 'earn their forgiveness' or to enter into some kind of transaction with God. Sometimes people made a pilgrimage in the hope that a relative would be released from prison or that their business or family might prosper.

The sixteenth-century writer Erasmus bemoaned the state of pilgrimages. He felt that they encouraged superstition and led many to believe that pilgrimage was a way of earning your salvation. He also condemned pilgrims for being immoral and for neglecting their homes while they were away. There can be no doubt that many pilgrimages were more of an excuse for a good holiday than for seeking God.

The end of this popular era of pilgrimage came swiftly and unexpectedly. Within a period of a few years, dramatic political changes began to take effect. It started when Henry VIII asserted his independence of the Church of Rome, and by 1534 the Reformation Parliament had made him head of the Church of England.

In 1538 he ordered the clergy to take down the images which filled many of their churches, and many of these pilgrim 'destinations' were destroyed for ever. In a matter of months the practice of pilgrimage declined rapidly, and people began to look elsewhere to fill this need.

Many people began to turn to the spas as destinations for healing and leisure. By the seventeenth-century people were travelling from all over Europe to spa towns like Harrogate and Bath in order to 'take the waters'.

The history of pilgrimage since the sixteenth-century has been one of increasing and decreasing popularity. The expansion of rail travel around 1850 made pilgrimage more popular, and cheaper air transport has had a similar effect more recently.

Nowadays people tend to go on pilgrimage in a group rather than alone, and many of today's pilgrims are quite young. Pilgrimages tend to be more and more ecumenical in nature, and they still bring together diverse groups of people from many different backgrounds.

The most popular destinations are Lourdes, with an annual total of three-million visitors, and Fatima, with two million. Several other French shrines receive more than a million pilgrims every year. Then there is Medjugorje in Yugoslavia. This is a great centre of present-day renewal for the Catholic (and wider) Church, with much emphasis on conversion, prayer, healing, reconciliation and world peace. It has a strong prophetic element. These pilgrimages usually have a strong devotional element and are generally organised by the Roman Catholic Church. Many people still look for healing on these pilgrimages, while others go to discover grace to cope with suffering.

One of the newest destinations for pilgrimage is Taizé in France. The Taizé Brotherhood shares its simple worship and ministry of reconciliation with thousands of pilgrims every year. This place has become the focus for the hopes and prayers of Christians all over the world.

Not every pilgrimage has just one destination. In Malta, for example, pilgrims walk to seven different churches on Maundy Thursday evening and because each church is a destination they may be visited in any order. The seven churches are all beautifully decorated, and each illustrates some aspect of the Passion of Christ. Pilgrims pause at each church to say their prayers, and I am told that there is a beautiful intensity in the worship.

The most popular destination for Christian pilgrimage is still Israel, and millions have visited the area in recent years. The political unrest hasn't stopped the flow of visitors, although some Christian groups resent the fact that pilgrims do not study the political situation as well as visit the holy places.

When I took a tour party to Israel a couple of years ago, we visited the different sites and read the relevant Bible verses. There was an intensity in the experience which I will never forget and several of our party said that their lives were profoundly affected by the experience.

The history of pilgrimage demonstrates that if we revere any particular place too much, we are in danger of making it our idol. A place may be important in leading us closer to the Lord, but it should always point towards a more important destination — the City of God.

Whatever the destination, it is important that our minds and hearts are focused on the Lord. During this last section of the pilgrimage, we begin to see our journey as a symbol of life itself. As we make our way towards the finishing point of our journey, our minds should turn to ultimate destinations and ultimate meanings.

Cardinal Basil Hume writes:

> Everything that is in me cries out for the need to reach a destination where there will be no more tears or pain, and where all my deepest aspirations and desires will be finally and completely satisfied. The thought of arriving at the place

> where all these things will be, and the thought of someone who will put it all right, that can keep me going. Every pilgrim cheerfully puts up with the journey when the going is rough, precisely because there is something to look forward to at the end of it.[1]

The promise that Jesus has gone to prepare a place for us has been a source of hope and joy to Christians everywhere. When we believe that 'all things are working together for good' we can see a glimmer of light, even in the darkest times.

One of the first prophets to articulate this message was Isaiah. He was writing from a hopeless situation. He was a prisoner in Babylon, Israel had fallen and the Temple was destroyed. He was surrounded by people who could see no hope and no future.

But into this dark despair he spoke a vision. He saw beyond the grief and dereliction of the Exile to the time when the watchmen on the city wall would see messengers coming over the horizon. He could hear their message. The Babylonian empire had fallen, and the people of Israel were free again. The messengers were declaring, 'Our God reigns!' The Israelites could go back home.

'Hark,' Isaiah wrote, 'your watchmen lift up their voice, together they sing for joy; for eye to eye they see the return of the Lord to Zion.'

His vision must have seemed like a fantasy. There was no sign of such a possibility. There were no messengers, and no watchmen shouting for joy. They were living in dark days. But eventually his prophecy was fulfilled. The messengers did appear. The promised news did arrive, and the people of Israel were able to go home.

At a time of hopelessness and despair, when there

seemed no future, Isaiah glimpsed God's perspective. He saw a vision of the future which could give them strength and courage in the midst of their troubles.

But scholars tell us that in Isaiah's prophecy there was a glimpse of an even greater victory. He could see beyond the struggles of his own time to the Lord's ultimate victory when evil would be removed for ever. Isaiah declared God's word to the people: 'I am making a new earth and new heavens. The events of the past will be completely forgotten.'

Isaiah's vision of God's eternal kingdom has been a source of hope and strength to countless Christians down the centuries. As we walk towards the end of the pilgrimage it is good to rejoice in the eternal destination that is ours.

This doctrine can affect our everyday life and give us a new perspective on the future. One day I was asked to visit a Christian lady who was suffering from deep depression. Her husband showed me into the darkened bedroom where she lay looking up at the ceiling. I sat on the bed beside her and read from my little pocket Bible, and I told her it was my prescription for her situation.

> Then I saw a new heaven and a new earth. . . I heard a loud voice speaking from the throne: 'Now God's home is with mankind! He will live with them, and they shall be his people. God himself will be with them, and He will be their God. He will wipe away all tears from their eyes. There will be no more death, no more grief or crying or pain. The old things have disappeared (Rev 21:1–4).

Even as I read I could sense something of her despair beginning to dissipate, and she began to see that in the goodness of God there was hope for the future. Months later she could look back and pinpoint that conversation as a turning-point in her recovery. In the depths of her despair she had glimpsed a New City, a place where suffering would be no more. Looking towards her ultimate destination from a distance was a great help and source of strength for her.

At this stage in the pilgrimage, we may be getting tired. We may have aching feet, particularly if we are not used to walking some distance. If it is a hot day we may be feeling particularly weary, and if it's raining we may have very muddy feet. It's the time on the journey when we may feel like giving up.

As we pause to rest, it might be helpful to remember the importance of keeping on and staying awake in life's pilgrimage. At all times we must be ready for our earthly journey to come to an end and our eternal destination to be reached.

When I was a teenager, I was a keen Sea Scout. I lived in Birmingham, so we used to sail on a local reservoir rather than on the sea. One summer, however, we rented a large two-masted Thames pilot cutter, and sailed across the North Sea and along the coast of Europe. We operated a watch system of 'four hours on' and 'four hours off'. This, together with the gale-force storms which lashed the boat night and day, was enough to send my mind reeling. It was a great experience, though I must confess to being more sea-sick than at any other time in my life!

One night I was on 'watch' from midnight to four am — the most wretched shift of all. Most of the crew were asleep, and it was my task to steer a steady course as I stared at the luminous green dial of the large marine compass. Unfortunately I fell fast asleep! I'd fought it for long enough, but at last my eyes closed and the boat ploughed on, following its own course.

I was awoken by a shuddering creak as this large vessel 'jibbed' and completely turned around. As the main boom mast swung across the deck it woke up the whole crew who appeared sleepily on the deck to see what on earth I'd done!

Many of us have lost direction in our lives and headed off course. No wonder Scripture says 'Wake up, sleeper!' So many of Christ's parables warn us to keep alert in 'the night watch'.

In the parable of the ten girls, the young ladies went to wait for the bridegroom so that they could join him in the great wedding celebration which would start when he arrived. He was very late and they all fell asleep. At midnight the cry was heard: 'The bridegroom's approaching', and all ten woke up. Five lamps were alight but the other five had run out of oil. They hadn't come prepared and went off to find more oil, but when they returned they'd missed the celebration.

'Be on your guard then', warned Jesus, 'because you do not know the day or the hour . . .' (Mt 25:13).

Jesus told another story about an owner-occupier who shut the door, drew the blinds and went to bed. It was just another night, and he expected no trouble.

When he woke up his house was ransacked and his possessions were gone. In the hours of darkness a thief had broken in and taken his goods. If the owner had known in advance he'd have hired a guard and set a trap. But no, he slept through the night watch.

'So then,' said Jesus, 'you must always be ready, because the Son of Man will come at an hour when you are not expecting him' (Mt 24:44).

Then we have the story of the servants who were waiting for their master to return from the wedding feast. They could have taken it easy, gone to sleep or sloped off home. But they remained faithful. At last the master came through the door, astonished to find them all awake and ready to serve him. He was so pleased that he made them sit down while he waited on them.

'And you too,' said Jesus 'must be ready, because the Son of Man will come at an hour when you are not expecting him.'

In these simple stories Jesus made it clear that those who choose to follow Him must always remain alert and prepared, because we may be called to 'give account' at any time.

One of the most difficult night watches I ever shared also turned out to be one of the most beautiful. Late one night I was called to a pleasant semi in a quiet South London street. The man I had gone to visit was in his mid-fifties and desperately ill.

He had endured many weary months as cancer had sapped his strength and invalided him out of the rat-race. Over those months we had shared many conversations about the meaning of life and as the reality of death drew closer, his faith had grown to meet it.

The duty doctor arrived, mobile-phone in hand, and told us that 'it wouldn't be long' before the patient was dead. His phone 'bleeped' and he disappeared into the dark windy night.

I was left in the darkened bedroom with my dying friend, and so began one of the most memorable conversations of my ministry. The wind gusted through the trees outside and I felt uneasy at the isolated situation I was facing.

My friend drifted from moments of lucidity to times when he sank into a coma. When he was able to talk he spoke with a perspective which only the deathbed can bring. He talked about his life and the signposts which had guided him down the years.

As he reflected on his life and his successful career with a large international corporation he concluded that in hindsight only three things held any significance. These were his faith, his family and his friends.

As the night drew on we talked more deeply about eternal life and the place which Jesus has prepared for us. As our conversation drew towards its end, I told him the story of *Pilgrim's Progress*, the famous allegory by John Bunyan, and the beautiful description of how Pilgrim crossed the River of Death.

Bunyan wrote:

> 'Now I further saw that between them and the gate was a river, but there was no bridge to go over, and the river was very deep. At the sight, therefore, of this river the pilgrims were much stunned; but the man that went with them said 'You must go through, or you cannot come at the gate. . . .
>
> Then they addressed themselves to the water and, entering, Christian began to sink; and crying out to his good friend Hopeful, he said, 'I sink in deep waters; the billows go over my head; all his waves go over me.'
>
> Then I saw in my dream that Christian was in a muse a while. To whom also Hopeful added this word — 'Be of good cheer, Jesus Christ maketh Thee whole.' And with that, Christian brake out with a loud voice, Oh, I see Him again! and he tells me, "When Thou passest through the waters, I will be with Thee; and through the rivers, they shall not overflow Thee." . . .
>
> Then they both took courage, and the enemy was, after that, as still as a stone, until they were gone over. Christian, therefore, presently found ground to stand upon; and so it followed that the rest of the river was but shallow; thus they got over.

Shortly after I had told this wonderful story to my friend, he died, and a great stillness descended on the room. A few minutes later the doctor looked in again to see how things were, and certified him dead.

As I reflected on my friend's last conversation, and his last journey across the river of death to the promised land, it made me examine my own priorities and see what was really important in my life.

Organising a church pilgrimage

Route eight: from the cross to the destination
Aim: to catch a vision of eternity and a new hope for the future.

If the route enables the group to glimpse their destination from a distance, it could be a very meaningful resting point, allowing them to consider the joy of the coming kingdom. As they look towards the destination in the distance, they could thank God for the coming kingdom and for the fact that Jesus has gone on to prepare a place for us.

This looking forwards is something which enriches our lives, enabling us to pray with joy at all times. Paul wrote to the Philippians, 'For what is life? To me, it is Christ. Death, then, will bring more.' Even in the darkest hour we can praise God for the life in heaven which awaits us; and as we pray for this suffering and divided world, we pray with an awareness that one day justice will prevail in the coming kingdom of the Lord.

At this resting-place there is time for personal petition and repentance. Individuals can recognise that one day they will have to meet their Maker, and that it is important for them to be right with him.

The final destination of the pilgrimage could be some historic or meaningful location. There is no shortage of destinations for pilgrimage here in Britain. Our nation's heritage is rich in the stories of men and women who have lived lives of faith, and it can be very helpful to visit the places where they lived and worked.

Although we should not worship those who've gone on before, it's good to remember them and learn from their experience. As the writer to the Hebrews said: 'Remember your leaders, who spoke the word of God to you. Consider the outcome of their way of life and imitate their faith (Heb 13:7–8).

People still make pilgrimages to the early missionary centres of Canterbury and Iona. Others visit Fountains Abbey in the Wye Valley or Mount Grace Priory in Yorkshire to remember the great tradition of prayer throughout our nation's history.

We can discover stories of people whose lives represent

part of the great 'household of faith' in many areas of the country. A pilgrimage in their footsteps can be an inspiring experience, making the destination something special.

John Bunyan, for example, was persecuted and imprisoned for twelve years. He wrote the Christian classic *Pilgrim's Progress* from Bedford Jail. His meeting-house and museum are in Bedford and might make a suitable destination.

Many people have made pilgrimages focusing on the life of John Wesley. They have recalled the story of his long struggle for faith, and his vision for the evangelisation of Britain. Destinations have included his birthplace at Epworth, his home in London's City Road or his New Room chapel in Bristol — all of which are open to the public. But as he travelled the country so extensively, he probably preached near your home.

Those living near Hull might like to make a journey to the Wilberforce Museum in the city centre. The Christian social reformer, William Wilberforce, fought slavery throughout his life until at last, in 1807, Parliament passed an act forbidding slave ships to enter British ports.

The missionary work of David Livingstone affected thousands of lives across Africa. Through his mission bases he taught the local people and cared for their needs. His life is well illustrated at the Livingstone Museum in Blantyre, Lanarkshire.

William Booth's vision for evangelism and social reform led to the formation of the Salvation Army. He had great practical concern for the poor, and this is illustrated in the Salvation Army Museum in Judd Street, London.

Other pilgrims may care to focus their attention on more contemporary issues. Their destination could be an area endangered by pollution, a military base, an area of racial tension or bad housing. Or it could be a visit to those who care for the poor or homeless today. On such a pilgrimage it is important that the political and social emphases don't overshadow the devotional element of the walk.

It isn't essential to have a special destination; in fact, it can be quite effective to make a pilgrimage to your home church and hold an act of worship there. If we pay too much attention to the physical destination, then it may overshadow the pilgrim walk itself.

At the end of the pilgrimage, we need to remember that it is only a symbol of our lifelong pilgrimage which leads to heaven. At the destination the leader may like to remind the pilgrims of the importance of committing themselves wholeheartedly to the Lord.

The famous Christian leader, Bishop Gore, used to preach to ordinands on the night before they were ordained into the Church of England. Every year he incorporated the same words into the conclusion of his sermon: 'Tomorrow I will say to you "Will you . . . will you? . . . will you? . . ." But one day another will ask . . . "Have you? . . . Have you? . . . Have you?"'

None of us know when we will have to face our Maker. We don't know the time or the hour when he will come back again, or call us to himself. So each of us must be ready to meet him, prepared to leave this earth to give account for the lives we've lived.

When the pilgrims arrive at the 'destination', they gather for a short time to sing and praise God for all that they've learnt on the journey.

Organising a personal pilgrimage

Personal prayer

Some Christians pray regularly for others, but rarely for themselves. It's important that we make space to reflect on our lives and pray for our needs. We must all confess our failure, ask God's forgiveness, seek his guidance and receive his renewing power. Although it's good to pray with other people, we should also spend time in prayer alone.

Preparation

Sometimes it's helpful to look back over recent days and reflect on the things we've thought, said and done. We'll quickly see ways in which we've hurt others and missed opportunities for caring. It can be meaningful to make a list of our faults, and confess the things we've done wrong one by one.

Activity

We look towards our destination, and remember that one day we must meet our Saviour face to face and give account for the way we've lived our lives.

Practical advice

(1) Whenever we come to the Lord in confession it's important to receive his forgiveness and love. John assures us: 'But if we confess our sins to God, he will keep his promise and do what is right: he will forgive us our sins and purify us from all our wrongdoing' 1 Jn 1:9. The Lord doesn't want us to live under condemnation, he wants to forgive and cleanse us.
(2) When we confess our sins to God, this may lead us to make amends for what we've done. We can't say sorry to

God for hurting another and avoid making a personal apology as well.
(3) In praying for ourselves we should be asking the Lord to break us, change us and mould us. In praying for ourselves we are asking the Lord to complete the work he's started in our lives.
(4) We should submit to him all our hopes and plans for the future, remembering that wherever he may lead us our destination is the City of God.
(5) We recognise in our prayers that even the most practical and mundane details of our lives are important to him, and that no aspect of our being is outside his care.

Personal follow-up

Prayer for ourselves is the most intense and personal kind of prayer. As we worship Jesus, love him, and submit our lives to him, we remember that one day we will meet him face to face and live with him for ever. Personal prayer is a preparation for glorious things to come.

Notes

1 Basil Hume, *To Be a Pilgrim* (SPCK: London, 1984).

Pilgrim song

Brian R. Hoare

2. We are learning, learning together,
Learning together on the pilgrim way.
Christ our Saviour, call us onward,
Onward together on the pilgrim way.

3. We are praying, praying together,
Praying together on the pilgrim way.
Holy Spirit, guide us upward,
Upward together on the pilgrim way.

4. We are growing, growing together,
Growing together on the pilgrim way.
Father, Son and Holy Spirit,
Draw us heavenward on the pilgrim way.

Breaking Bread

by Rob Frost

Holy Communion is probably the supreme focus of Christian worship. As such it is the centre from which our whole life can be transformed. This book explores the nature of our worship, its mystery and its contemporary relevance.

'To come to grips with this book must mean richer worship. Here is the background and the theology, the workshop ideas, discussion starters and practical study sessions. The experience of hundreds of worship workshops packed into stimulating sessions for housegroups, church councils or conferences.'

– *David Martin (General Secretary Designate, Methodist Association of Youth Clubs)*

'This is a stimulating book, which puts worship at the centre of Christian life and will help people of all ages and all traditions to renew their worship.'

– *Rev David Calvert (Chairman of the Methodist Church, York and Hull District)*

'Rob Frost travels fast and far, missing little on the journey. He drives with the windows open, so fresh air blows everywhere.'

– *Dr Donald English (former Moderator of the Free Church Federal Council)*

Rob Frost works for the Methodist Home Mission division and the Methodist Association of Youth Clubs. He conducts many evangelistic missions and organised the musicals *Daybreak* and *Visions*.

Kingsway Publications

Intimate Friendship with God

by Joy Dawson

'Every person is either fulfilled or frustrated to the degree he or she is in intimate friendship with God.'

Can we really know God as an intimate friend? And if so, what is the key to such a relationship?

At a time when so many are after instant gratification, Joy Dawson reminds us of 'the fear of the Lord'. This, she says, is the hallmark of intimate friendship with God. As we learn to love the truth that He loves, and to hate the sin that He hates, we become recognizable as His people. We begin to 'delight in holiness'. And He delights in us . . .

The price is high, but the privileges and rewards still higher.

Joy Dawson has taught with Youth With A Mission in over forty countries and her ministry has been enjoyed by thousands seeking a deeper experience of God. She and her husband Jim have two married children.

Kingsway Publications

Bible Meditation

by Alex Buchanan

A life centred on God—an elusive dream, or a daily reality?

Alex Buchanan believes that it is possible to know the peace, guidance and joy of God's presence day by day. We in the West starve ourselves when we have an ample supply of food all around us—God's written word.

This book shows that meditating on Scripture can be one of life's most rewarding and exciting experiences, opening the door to heavenly riches—as long as we refuse to adopt the world's get-rich-quick mentality. More than that, we see how Spirit-filled prophecy and an effective prayer life flow out of the new dimension that Bible meditation brings to those who won't settle for anything less.

Kingsway Publications

Come into His Presence

by John Wallis

Everyone seems to agree that prayer is at the heart of the Christian life—as essential as the air we breathe—but how many Christians actually enjoy prayer?

This book has been written to remind us just how exciting prayer can be. John Wallis has seen what has happened in Korea and other parts of Asia when Christians take prayer seriously, and he longs for a similar dedication in the hearts of Christians in the West.

In a series of short chapters the author gives practical suggestions on a wide variety of issues related to both individual and corporate prayer.

John Wallis is the Director of the Overseas Missionary Fellowship in the UK.

Kingsway Publications